The Light of Asia

or

The Great Renunciation

(Mahâbhinishkramana)

Being

The Life and Teaching of Gautama

Prince of India and founder of Buddhism

The Light of Asia

or

The Great Renunciation

(Mahâbhinishkramana)

Being The Life and Teaching of Gautama
Prince of India and Founder of Buddhism
(As Told in Verse by an Indian Buddhist)

Edwin Arnold

Low Price Publications

Low Price Publications
2015

Edwin Arnold (1832-1904)

First Published 1879
This Impression reproduced from the Edition published in 1892
Reprinted in **LPP** 2000, 2010, 2015

ISBN 10: 81-7536-509-9
ISBN 13: 978-81-7536-509-4

Published by
Low Price Publications
A-6, 2nd Floor, Nimri Commercial Centre,
Ashok Vihar Phase 4, Delhi 110052 (INDIA)
tel.: +91-11-27302453 fax.: +91-11-47061936
url: www.LPPindia.com e-mail: info@LPPindia.com

Printed at
Balaji Offset, Delhi

PRINTED IN INDIA

THE

Light of Asia

OR

THE GREAT RENUNCIATION

(MAHABHINISHKRAMANA).

BEING

THE LIFE AND TEACHING OF GAUTAMA

PRINCE OF INDIA AND FOUNDER OF BUDDHISM

(As Told in Verse by an Indian Buddhist).

BY

SIR EDWIN ARNOLD,

M.A., K.C.I.E., C.S.I.

A New Edition.

LONDON:

KEGAN PAUL, TRENCH, TRÜBNER, & CO., LTD

1892

This Volume

IS DUTIFULLY INSCRIBED TO

The Sovereign, Grand Master, and Companions

OF

The Most Exalted Order of the Star of India

BY

THE AUTHOR.

PUBLISHERS' NOTICE.

SINCE its original appearance the "Light of Asia" has passed through a very large series of editions, and the demand seems at the present moment to be increasing rather than diminishing. An extraordinary number of copies in various forms have been sold here at prices from a guinea downwards, exclusive of the various authorised and unauthorised issues which have appeared in America, and have found their way very largely into the Indian and Colonial market. There have appeared also translations of the poem into almost every European and numerous Oriental languages, and it may probably be claimed for it that many people otherwise well-read and educated would never have had more than the faintest notion of the exquisite beauties of the Buddhistic faith, had they not been presented to them in so delightful and at the same time so accurate a form as by the "Light of Asia." By reason of its enormous popularity in the Christian world, and because it has become a religious guide-book for the pious Buddhist, the publishers are encouraged in the present issue to give the "Light of Asia" outwardly also a popular and artistic dress. The illustrations in the present volume are taken chiefly from Buddhist sculptures and frescoes of an average age of 2000 years, and if in some instances the rudeness of design and strangeness of conception may not immediately commend themselves to the Western eye, they will nevertheless be helpful in portraying the inner spirit of an ancient culture which produced one of the great living religions of the present day.

TRÜBNER & CO.

October 1889.

PREFACE.

IN the following Poem I have sought, by the medium of an imaginary Buddhist votary, to depict the life and character and indicate the philosophy of that noble hero and reformer, Prince Gautama of India, the founder of Buddhism.

A generation ago little or nothing was known in Europe of this great faith of Asia, which had nevertheless existed during twenty-four centuries, and at this day surpasses, in the number of its followers and the area of its prevalence, any other form of creed. Four hundred and seventy millions of our race live and die in the tenets of Gautama; and the spiritual dominions of this ancient teacher extend, at the present time, from Nepaul and Ceylon, over the whole

Eastern Peninsula, to China, Japan, Thibet, Central Asia, Siberia, and even Swedish Lapland. India itself might fairly be included in this magnificent Empire of Belief; for though the profession of Buddhism has for the most part passed away from the land of its birth, the mark of Gautama's sublime teaching is stamped ineffaceably upon modern Brahmanism, and the most characteristic habits and convictions of the Hindus are clearly due to the benign influence of Buddha's precepts. More than a third of mankind, therefore, owe their moral and religious ideas to this illustrious prince; whose personality, though imperfectly revealed in the existing sources of information, cannot but appear the highest, gentlest, holiest, and most beneficent, with one exception, in the history of Thought. Discordant in frequent particulars, and sorely overlaid by corruptions, inventions, and misconceptions, the Buddhistical books yet agree in the one point of recording nothing—no single act or word—which mars the perfect purity and tenderness of this Indian teacher, who united the truest princely qualities with the intellect of a sage and the passionate devotion of a martyr. Even M. Barthélemy St. Hilaire, totally misjudging as he does, many points of Buddhism, is well cited by Professor Max Müller as saying of Prince Siddârtha, "Sa vie n'a point de tache. Son constant héroïsme égale sa conviction; et si la théorie qu'il préconise est fausse, les exemples personnels qu'il donne sont irréprochables. Il est le modèle achevé de toutes les vertus qu'il prêche; son abnégation, sa charité, son inaltérable douceur ne se démentent point un seul instant. . . . Il prépare silencieusment sa doctrine par six années de retraite et de méditation; il la propage par la seule puissance de la parole et de la persuasion pendant plus d'un demi-siècle, et quand il meurt entre les bras de ses disciples, c'est avec la sérénité d'un sage qui a pratiqué le bien toute sa vie, et qui est assuré d'avoir trouvé le vrai." To Gautama has consequently been granted this stupendous conquest of humanity; and—though he discountenanced ritual, and declared himself, even when on the threshold of Nirvana, to be only what all other men might become—the love and gratitude of Asia, disobeying his mandate, have given him fervent worship. Forests of flowers are daily laid upon his stainless shrines, and countless millions of lips daily repeat the formula "I take refuge in Buddha!"

The Buddha of this poem—if, as need not be doubted, he really existed—was born on the borders of Nepaul about 620 B.C., and died about 543 B.C. at Kusinagara in Oudh. In point of age, therefore, most other creeds are youthful compared with this venerable religion, which has in it the eternity of a universal hope, the immortality of a boundless love, an indestructible element of faith in final good, and the proudest assertion ever made of human freedom. The extravagances which disfigure the record and practice of Buddhism are to be referred to that inevitable degradation which priesthoods always inflict upon great ideas committed to their charge. The power and sublimity of Gautama's original doctrines should be estimated by their influence, not by their interpreters; nor by that innocent but lazy and ceremonious church which has arisen on the foundations of the Buddhistic Brotherhood or "Sangha."

I have put my poem into a Buddhist's mouth, because, to appreciate the spirit of Asiatic thoughts, they should be regarded from the Oriental point of view; and neither the miracles which consecrate this record, nor the philosophy which it embodies, could have been otherwise so naturally reproduced. The doctrine of Transmigration, for instance—startling to modern minds—was established and thoroughly accepted by the Hindus of Buddha's time; that period when Jerusalem was being taken by Nebuchadnezzar, when Nineveh was falling to the Medes, and Marseilles was founded by the Phocæans. The exposition here offered of so antique a system is of necessity incomplete, and—in obedience to the laws of poetic art—passes rapidly by many matters philosophically most important, as well as over the long ministry of Gautama. But my purpose has been obtained if any just conception be here conveyed of the lofty character of this noble prince, and of the general purport of his doctrines. As to these latter there has arisen prodigious controversy among the erudite, who will be aware that I have taken the imperfect Buddhistic citations much as they stand in Spence Hardy's work, and have also modified more than one passage in the received narratives. The views, however, here indicated of "Nirvana," "Dharma," "Karma," and the other chief features of Buddhism, are at least the fruits of considerable study, and also of a firm conviction that a third of mankind would never have been brought to believe in blank abstractions, or in Nothingness as the issue and crown of Being.

Finally, in reverence to the illustrious Promulgator of this "Light of Asia," and in homage to the many eminent scholars who have devoted noble labours to his memory, for which both repose and ability are wanting to me, I beg that the shortcomings of my too-hurried study may be forgiven. It has been composed in the brief intervals of days without leisure, but is inspired by an abiding desire to aid in the better mutual knowledge of East and West. The time may come, I hope, when this book and my "Indian Song of Songs," and "Indian Idylls," will preserve the memory of one who loved India and the Indian peoples.

EDWIN ARNOLD.

LIST OF ILLUSTRATIONS.

BOOK I.

BOOK II.

BOOK III.

BOOK IV.

BOOK V.

BOOK VI.

BOOK VII.

BOOK VIII.

BOOK THE FIRST.

BUDDHA.

[From a sculpture found in Gāndhāra (Yuzufzai).

Book the First.

THE Scripture of the Saviour of the World,
Lord Buddha—Prince Siddârtha styled on earth—
In Earth and Heavens and Hells Incomparable,
All-honoured, Wisest, Best, most Pitiful;
The Teacher of Nirvâna and the Law.

Thus came he to be born again for men.

Below the highest sphere four Regents sit
Who rule our world; and under them are zones
Nearer, but high, where saintliest spirits dead
Wait thrice ten thousand years, then live again;
And on Lord Buddha, waiting in that sky,

Came for our sakes the five sure signs of birth,
So that the Devas knew the signs, and said
"Buddha will go again to help the World."
"Yea!" spake He, "now I go to help the World
This last of many times; for birth and death
End hence for me and those who learn my Law.
I will go down among the Sâkyas,
Under the southward snows of Himalay,
Where pious people live and a just King."

That night the wife of King Suddhôdana,
Maya the Queen, asleep beside her Lord,
Dreamed a strange dream; dreamed that a star from
heaven—
Splendid, six-rayed, in colour rosy-pearl,
Whereof the token was an Elephant
Six-tusked, and white as milk of Kamadhuk—
Shot through the void; and, shining into her,
Entered her womb upon the right. Awaked,
Bliss beyond mortal mother's filled her breast,
And over half the earth a lovely light
Forewent the morn. The strong hills shook; the waves
Sank lulled; all flowers that blow by day came forth
As 'twere high noon; down to the farthest hells
Passed the Queen's joy, as when warm sunshine thrills

Wood-glooms to gold, and into all the deeps
A tender whisper pierced. "Oh ye," it said,
"The dead that are to live, the live who die,
Uprise, and hear, and hope! Buddha is come!"
Whereat in Limbos numberless much peace
Spread, and the world's heart throbbed, and a wind
blew
With unknown freshness over lands and seas.
And when the morning dawned, and this was told,
The grey dream-readers said "The dream is good!
The Crab is in conjunction with the Sun;
The Queen shall bear a boy, a holy child
Of wondrous wisdom, profiting all flesh,
Who shall deliver men from ignorance,
Or rule the world, if he will deign to rule."

In this wise was the holy Buddha born.

Queen Maya stood at noon, her days fulfilled,
Under a Palsa in the Palace-grounds,
A stately trunk, straight as a temple-shaft,
With crown of glossy leaves and fragrant blooms;
And, knowing the time come—for all things knew—
The conscious tree bent down its bows to make
A bower about Queen Maya's majesty;

And Earth put forth a thousand sudden flowers
To spread a couch; while, ready for the bath,
The rock hard by gave out a limpid stream
Of crystal flow. So brought she forth her child
Pangless—he having on his perfect form
The marks, thirty and two, of blessed birth;
Of which the great news to the Palace came.
But when they brought the painted palanquin
To fetch him home, the bearers of the poles
Were the four Regents of the Earth, come down
From Mount Sumeru—they who write men's deeds
On brazen plates—the Angel of the East,
Whose hosts are clad in silver robes, and bear
Targèts of pearl: the Angel of the South,
Whose horsemen, the Kumbhandas, ride blue steeds,
With sapphire shields: the Angel of the West,
By Nâgas followed, riding steeds blood-red,
With coral shields: the Angel of the North,
Environed by his Yakshas, all in gold,
On yellow horses, bearing shields of gold.
These, with their pomp invisible, came down
And took the poles, in cast and outward garb
Like bearers, yet most mighty gods; and gods
Walked free with men that day, though men knew not:

For Heaven was filled with gladness for Earth's sake,
Knowing Lord Buddha thus was come again.

But King Suddhôdana wist not of this;
The portents troubled, till his dream-readers
Augured a Prince of earthly dominance,
A Chakravartîn, such as rise to rule
Once in each thousand years; seven gifts he has—

The Chakra-ratna, disc divine; the gem;
The horse, the Aswa-ratna, that proud steed
Which tramps the clouds; a snow-white elephant,
The Hasti-ratna, born to bear his King;

The crafty Minister, the General
Unconquered, and the wife of peerless grace,
The Istrî-ratna, lovelier than the Dawn.
For which gifts looking with this wondrous boy,
The King gave order that his town should keep
High festival; therefore the ways were swept,
Rose-odours sprinkled in the street, the trees
Were hung with lamps and flags, while merry crowds
Gaped on the sword-players and posturers,
The jugglers, charmers, swingers, rope-walkers,
The nautch-girls in their spangled skirts, and bells
That chime light laughter round their restless feet;
The masquers wrapped in skins of bear and deer,
The tiger-tamers, wrestlers, quail-fighters,
Beaters of drum and twanglers of the wire,

Who made the people happy by command.
Moreover, from afar came merchant-men,
Bringing, on tidings of this birth, rich gifts
In golden trays; goat-shawls, and nard, and jade,

Turkises, "evening-sky" tint, woven webs—
So fine twelve folds hide not a modest face—
Waist-cloths sewn thick with pearls, and sandal-wood;
Homage from tribute cities; so they called
Their Prince Savârthasiddh, "All-Prospering,"
Briefer, Siddârtha.

'Mongst the strangers came
A grey-haired saint, Asita, one whose ears,
Long closed to earthly things, caught heavenly sounds,
And heard at prayer beneath his peepul-tree
The Devas singing songs at Buddha's birth.
Wondrous in lore he was by age and fasts;
Him, drawing nigh, seeming so reverend,
The King saluted, and Queen Maya made
To lay her babe before such holy feet;
But when he saw the Prince the old man cried
"Ah, Queen, not so!" and thereupon he touched
Eight times the dust, laid his waste visage there,
Saying, "O Babe! I worship! Thou art He!
I see the rosy light, the foot-sole marks,
The soft curled tendril of the Swastika,
The sacred primal signs thirty and two,
The eighty lesser tokens. Thou art Buddh,
And thou wilt preach the Law and save all flesh
Who learn the Law, though I shall never hear,

Dying too soon, who lately longed to die ;
Howbeit I have seen Thee. Know, O King !
This is that Blossom on our human tree
Which opens once in many myriad years—
But opened, fills the world with Wisdom's scent
And Love's dropped honey ; from thy royal root
A Heavenly Lotus springs : Ah, happy House !
Yet not all-happy, for a sword must pierce
Thy bowels for this boy—whilst thou, sweet Queen !
Dear to all gods and men for this great birth,
Henceforth art grown too sacred for more woe ;
And life is woe, therefore in seven days
Painless thou shalt attain the close of pain."

Which fell : for on the seventh evening
Queen Maya smiling slept, and waked no more,
Passing content to Trâyastrinshas-Heaven,
Where countless Devas worship her, and wait
Attendant on that radiant Motherhead.
But for the Babe they found a foster-nurse,
Princess Mahâprajâpati—her breast
Nourished with noble milk the lips of Him
Whose lips comfort the worlds.

When th' eighth year passed,
The careful King bethought to teach his son

All that a Prince should learn, for still he shunned
The too vast presage of those miracles,
The glories and the sufferings of a Buddh.
So, in full council of his Ministers,
"Who is the wisest man, great sirs," he asked,
"To teach my Prince that which a Prince should
    know?"
Whereto gave answer each with instant voice:
"King! Viswamitra is the wisest one,
The farthest-seen in Scriptures, and the best
In learning, and the manual arts, and all."
Thus Viswamitra came and heard commands;
And, on a day found fortunate, the Prince
Took up his slate of ox-red sandal-wood
All beautified by gems around the rim,
And sprinkled smooth with dust of emery,
These took he, and his writing-stick, and stood
With eyes bent down before the Sage, who said,
"Child, write this Scripture," speaking slow the verse
"*Gâyatrî*" named, which only High-born hear:—

Om, tatsaviturvareṇyam
Bhargo devasya dhîmahi
Dhiyo yo na prachodayât.

"Acharya, I write," meekly replied

The Prince, and quickly on the dust he drew—
Not in one script, but many characters—
The sacred verse ; Nagri and Dakshin, Nî,
Mangal, Parusha, Yava, Tirthi, Uk,
Darad, Sikhyani, Mana, Madhyachar,
The pictured writings and the speech of signs,
Tokens of cave men and the sea-peoples,
Of those who worship snakes beneath the earth,
And those who flame adore and the sun's orb,
The Magians and the dwellers on the mounds ;
Of all the nations all strange scripts he traced
One after other with his writing-stick,
Reading the master's verse in every tongue ;
And Viswamitra said, "It is enough,
Let us to numbers.
After me repeat
Your numeration till we reach the Lakh,
One, two, three, four, to ten, and then by tens
To hundreds, thousands." After him the child
Named digits, decads, centuries ; nor paused,
The round lakh reached, but softly murmured on,
"Then comes the kôti, nahut, ninnahut,
Khamba, viskhamba, abab, attata,
To kumuds, gundhikas, and utpalas,
By pundarîkas unto padumas,

Which last is how you count the utmost grains
Of Hastagiri ground to finest dust;
But beyond that a numeration is,
The Kâtha, used to note the stars of night;
The Kôti-Kâtha, for the ocean drops;
Ingga, the calculus of circulars;
Sarvanikchepa, by the which you deal
With all the sands of Gunga, till we come
To Antah-Kalpas, where the unit is
The sands of ten crore Gungas. If one seeks
More comprehensive scale, th' arithmic mounts
By the Asankya, which is the tale
Of all the drops that in ten thousand years
Would fall on all the worlds by daily rain;
Thence unto Maha-Kalpas, by the which
The Gods compute their future and their past."

"'Tis good," the sage rejoined. "Most noble Prince,
If these thou know'st, needs it that I should teach
The mensuration of the lineal?"
Humbly the boy replied, "Acharya!
Be pleased to hear me. Paramânus ten
A parasukshma make; ten of those build
The trasarene, and seven trasarenes
One mote's-length floating in the beam, seven motes

The whisker-point of mouse, and ten of these
One likhya ; likhyas ten a yuka, ten
Yukas a heart of barley, which is held
Seven times a wasp-waist ; so unto the grain
Of mung and mustard and the barley-corn,
Whereof ten give the finger-joint, twelve joints
The span, wherefrom we reach the cubit, staff,
Bow-length, lance-length ; while twenty lengths of lance
Mete what is named a 'breath,' which is to say
Such space as man may stride with lungs once filled,
Whereof a gow is forty, four times that
A yôjana ; and, Master ! if it please,
I shall recite how many sun-motes lie
From end to end within a yôjana."
Thereat, with instant skill, the little Prince
Pronounced the total of the atoms true.
But Viswamitra heard it on his face
Prostrate before the boy ; "For thou," he cried,
"Art Teacher of thy teachers—thou, not I,
Art Gûrû. Oh, I worship thee, sweet Prince !
That comest to my school only to show
Thou knowest all without the books, and know'st
Fair reverence besides."

Which reverence
Lord Buddha kept to all his schoolmasters,

Albeit beyond their learning taught; in speech
Right gentle, yet so wise; princely of mien,
Yet softly-mannered; modest, deferent,
And tender-hearted, though of fearless blood;
No bolder horseman in the youthful band
E'er rode in gay chase of the shy gazelles;
No keener driver of the chariot
In mimic contest scoured the Palace-courts;
Yet in mid-play the boy would ofttimes pause,
Letting the deer pass free; would ofttimes yield
His half-won race because the labouring steeds
Fetched painful breath; or if his princely mates
Saddened to lose, or if some wistful dream
Swept o'er his thoughts. And ever with the years
Waxed this compassionateness of our Lord,
Even as a great tree grows from two soft leaves
To spread its shade afar; but hardly yet
Knew the young child of sorrow, pain, or tears,
Save as strange names for things not felt by kings,
Nor ever to be felt. Then it befell
In the Royal garden on a day of spring,
A flock of wild swans passed, voyaging north
To their nest-places on Himâla's breast.
Calling in love-notes down their snowy line
The bright birds flew, by fond love piloted;

And Devadatta, cousin of the Prince,
Pointed his bow, and loosed a wilful shaft
Which found the wide wing of the foremost swan
Broad-spread to glide upon the free blue road,
So that it fell, the bitter arrow fixed,
Bright scarlet blood-gouts staining the pure plumes.
Which seeing, Prince Siddârtha took the bird
Tenderly up, rested it in his lap—
Sitting with knees crossed, as Lord Buddha sits—
And, soothing with a touch the wild thing's fright,
Composed its ruffled vans, calmed its quick heart,
Caressed it into peace with light kind palms
As soft as plantain-leaves an hour unrolled;
And while the left hand held, the right hand drew
The cruel steel forth from the wound, and laid
Cool leaves and healing honey on the smart.
Yet all so little knew the boy of pain
That curiously into his wrist he pressed
The arrow's barb, and winced to feel it sting,
And turned with tears to soothe his bird again.

Then some one came who said, "My Prince hath shot
A swan, which fell among the roses here,
He bids me pray you send it. Will you send?"

"Nay," quoth Siddârtha, "if the bird were dead
To send it to the slayer might be well,
But the swan lives; my cousin hath but killed
The god-like speed which throbbed in this white wing."
And Devadatta answered, "The wild thing,
Living or dead, is his who fetched it down;
'Twas no man's in the clouds, but fall'n 'tis mine.
Give me my prize, fair Cousin." Then our Lord
Laid the swan's neck beside his own smooth cheek
And gravely spake, "Say no! the bird is mine,
The first of myriad things which shall be mine
By right of mercy and love's lordliness.
For now I know, by what within me stirs,
That I shall teach compassion unto men
And be a speechless world's interpreter,
Abating this accursed flood of woe,
Not man's alone; but, if the Prince disputes,
Let him submit his matter to the wise
And we will wait their word." So was it done;
In full divan the business had debate,
And many thought this thing and many that;
Till there arose an unknown priest who said,
"If life be aught, the saviour of a life
Owns more the living thing than he can own
Who sought to slay—the slayer spoils and wastes,

The cherisher sustains; give him the bird:"
Which judgment all found just; but when the King
Sought out the sage for honour, he was gone,
And some one saw a hooded snake glide forth,—
The gods come ofttimes thus! So our Lord Buddh
Began his works of mercy.

Yet not more
Knew he as yet of grief than that one bird's,
Which, being healed, went joyous to its kind.
But on another day the King said, "Come,
Sweet son! and see the pleasaunce of the spring,
And how the fruitful earth is wooed to yield
Its riches to the reaper; how my realm—
Which shall be thine when the pile flames for me—
Feeds all its mouths and keeps the King's chest filled.
Fair is the season with new leaves, bright blooms,
Green grass, and cries of plough-time." So they rode
Into a land of wells and gardens, where,
All up and down the rich red loam, the steers
Strained their strong shoulders in the creaking yoke
Dragging the ploughs; the fat soil rose and rolled
In smooth long waves back from the plough; who drove
Planted both feet upon the leaping share
To make the furrow deep; among the palms

The tinkle of the rippling water rang,
And where it ran the glad earth 'broidered it
With balsams and the spears of lemon-grass.
Elsewhere were sowers who went forth to sow;
And all the jungle laughed with nesting-songs,
And all the thickets rustled with small life
Of lizard, bee, beetle, and creeping things
Pleased at the spring-time. In the mango-sprays
The sun-birds flashed; alone at his green forge
Toiled the loud coppersmith; bee eaters hawked,
Chasing the purple butterflies; beneath,
Striped squirrels raced, the mynas perked and picked.
The seven brown sisters chattered in the thorn,
The pied fish-tiger hung above the pool,
The egrets stalked among the buffaloes,
The kites sailed circles in the golden air;
About the painted temple peacocks flew,
The blue doves cooed from every well, far off
The village drums beat for some marriage-feast;
All things spoke peace and plenty, and the Prince
Saw and rejoiced. But, looking deep, he saw
The thorns which grow upon this rose of life:
How the swart peasant sweated for his wage,
Toiling for leave to live: and how he urged
The great-eyed oxen through the flaming hours,

Goading their velvet flanks: then marked he, too,
How lizard fed on ant, and snake on him,
And kite on both; and how the fish-hawk robbed
The fish-tiger of that which it had seized;
The shrike chasing the bulbul, which did hunt
The jewelled butterflies; till everywhere
Each slew a slayer and in turn was slain,
Life living upon death. So the fair show
Veiled one vast, savage, grim conspiracy
Of mutual murder, from the worm to man,
Who himself kills his fellow; seeing which—
The hungry ploughman and his labouring kine,
Their dewlaps blistered with the bitter yoke,
The rage to live which makes all living strife—
The Prince Siddârtha sighed. "Is this," he said,
"That happy earth they brought me forth to see?
How salt with sweat the peasant's bread! how hard
The oxen's service! in the brake how fierce
The war of weak and strong! i' th' air what plots!
No refuge e'en in water. Go aside
A space, and let me muse on what ye show."

So saying the good Lord Buddha seated him
Under a jambu-tree, with ankles crossed—
As holy statues sit—and first began

To meditate this deep disease of life,
What its far source and whence its remedy.
So vast a pity filled him, such wide love
For living things, such passion to heal pain,
That by their stress his princely spirit passed
To ecstasy, and, purged from mortal taint
Of sense and self, the boy attained thereat
Dhyâna, first step of "the path."
There flew
High overhead that hour five holy ones,

Whose free wings faltered as they passed the tree.
"What power superior draws us from our flight?"
They asked,—for spirits feel all force divine,
And know the sacred presence of the pure.
Then, looking downward, they beheld the Buddh

Crowned with a rose-hued aureole, intent
On thoughts to save; while from the grove a voice
Cried, "Rishis! this is He shall help the world,
Descend and worship." So the Bright Ones came
And sang a song of praise, folding their wings;
Then journeyed on, taking good news to Gods.

But certain from the King seeking the Prince
Found him still musing, though the noon was past,
And the sun hastened to the western hills:
Yet, while all shadows moved, the jambu-tree's
Stayed in one quarter, overspreading him,
Lest the sloped rays should strike that sacred head;
And he who saw this sight heard a voice say,
Amid the blossoms of the rose-apple,
"Let be the King's son! till the shadow goes
Forth from his heart my shadow will not shift."

BOOK THE SECOND.

Book the Second.

NOW, when our Lord was come to eighteen years,
The King commanded that there should be built
Three stately houses, one of hewn square beams
With cedar lining, warm for winter days ;
One of veined marbles, cool for summer heat ;
And one of burned bricks, with blue tiles bedecked,
Pleasant at seed-time, when the champaks bud—
Subha, Suramma, Ramma, were their names.
Delicious gardens round about them bloomed,
Streams wandered wild, and musky thickets stretched,
With many a bright pavilion and fair lawn,
In midst of which Siddârtha strayed at will,
Some new delight provided every hour ;
And happy hours he knew, for life was rich,

With youthful blood at quickest; yet still came
The shadows of his meditation back,
As the lake's silver dulls with driving clouds.

Which the King marking, called his Ministers:
"Bethink ye, sirs! how the old Rishi spake,"
He said, "and what my dream-readers foretold.
This boy, more dear to me than mine heart's blood,
Shall be of universal dominance,
Trampling the neck of all his enemies,
A King of kings—and this is in my heart;—
Or he shall tread the sad and lowly path
Of self-denial and of pious pains,
Gaining who knows what good, when all is lost
Worth keeping; and to this his wistful eyes
Do still incline amid my palaces.
But ye are sage, and ye will counsel me;
How may his feet be turned to that proud road
Where they should walk, and all fair signs come true
Which gave him Earth to rule, if he would rule?"

The eldest answered, "Maharaja! love
Will cure these thin distempers; weave the spell
Of woman's wiles about his idle heart.
What knows this noble boy of beauty yet,

Eyes that make heaven forgot, and lips of balm?
Find him soft wives and pretty playfellows;
The thoughts ye cannot stay with brazen chains
A girl's hair lightly binds."

And all thought good.

But the King answered, "If we seek him wives,
Love chooseth ofttimes with another eye;
And if we bid range Beauty's garden round,
To pluck what blossom pleases, he will smile
And sweetly shun the joy he knows not of."
Then said another, "Roams the barasingh
Until the fated arrow flies; for him,
As for less lordly spirits, some one charms,
Some face will seem a Paradise, some form
Fairer than pale Dawn when she wakes the world.
This do, my King! Command a festival
Where the realm's maids shall be competitors
In youth and grace, and sports that Sâkyas use.
Let the Prince give the prizes to the fair,
And, when the lovely victors pass his seat,
There shall be those who mark if one or two
Change the fixed sadness of his tender cheek;
So we may chose for Love with Love's own eyes,
And cheat his Highness into happiness."
This thing seemed good; wherefore, upon a day,

The criers bade the young and beautiful
Pass to the palace, for 'twas in command
To hold a court of pleasure, and the Prince
Would give the prizes, something rich for all,
The richest for the fairest judged. Thus flocked
Kapilavastu's maidens to the gate,
Each with her dark hair newly smoothed and bound,
Eyelashes lustred with the soorma-stick,
Fresh-bathed and scented; all in shawls and cloths
Of gayest; slender hands and feet new-stained
With crimson, and the tilka-spots stamped bright.
Fair show it was of all those Indian girls
Slow-pacing past the throne with large black eyes
Fixed on the ground; for when they saw the Prince
More than the awe of Majesty made beat
Their fluttering hearts, he sate so passionless,
Gentle, but so beyond them. Each maid took
With down-dropped lids her gift, afraid to gaze;
And if the people hailed some lovelier one
Beyond her rivals worthy royal smiles,
She stood like a scared antelope to touch
The gracious hand, then fled to join her mates
Trembling at favour, so divine he seemed,
So high and saint-like and above her world.
Thus filed they, one bright maid after another,

The city's flowers, and all this beauteous march
Was ending and the prizes spent, when last
Came young Yasôdhara, and they that stood
Nearest Siddârtha saw the princely boy
Start, as the radiant girl approached. A form
Of heavenly mould; a gait like Parvati's;
Eyes like a hind's in love-time; face so fair
Words cannot paint its spell; and she alone
Gazed full—folding her palms across her breasts—
On the boy's gaze, her stately neck unbent.
"Is there a gift for me?" she asked, and smiled.
"The gifts are gone," the Prince replied, "yet take
This for amends, dear sister, of whose grace
Our happy city boasts;" therewith he loosed
The emerald necklet from his throat, and clasped
Its green beads round her dark and silk-soft waist;
And their eyes mixed, and from the look sprang
love.

Long after—when enlightenment was full—
Lord Buddha, being prayed why thus his heart
Took fire at first glance of the Sâkya girl,
Answered, "We were not strangers, as to us
And all it seemed; in ages long gone by
A hunter's son, playing with forest girls

By Yamun's springs, where Nandadevi stands,
Sate umpire while they raced beneath the firs
Like hares at eve that run their playful rings;
One with flower-stars he crowned; one with long plumes
Plucked from eyed pheasant and the jungle-cock;
One with fir-apples; but who ran the last
Came first for him, and unto her the boy
Gave a tame fawn and his heart's love beside.
And in the wood they lived many glad years,
And in the wood they undivided died.
Lo! as hid seed shoots after rainless years,
So good and evil, pains and pleasures, hates
And loves, and all dead deeds, come forth again
Bearing bright leaves or dark, sweet fruit or sour.
Thus I was he and she Yasôdhara;
And while the wheel of birth and death turns round
That which hath been must be between us two."

But they who watched the Prince at prize-giving
Saw and heard all, and told the careful King
How sate Siddârtha heedless, till there passed
Great Suprabuddha's child, Yasôdhara;
And how—at sudden sight of her—he changed,
And how she gazed on him and he on her,

And of the jewel-gift, and what beside
Passed in their speaking glance.
The fond King smiled:
"Look! we have found a lure; take counsel now
To fetch therewith our falcon from the clouds.
Let messengers be sent to ask the maid
In marriage for my son." But it was law
With Sâkyas, when any asked a maid
Of noble house, fair and desirable,
He must make good his skill in martial arts
Against all suitors who should challenge it;
Nor might this custom break itself for kings.
Therefore her father spake: "Say to the King,
The child is sought by princes far and near;
If thy most gentle son can bend the bow,
Sway sword, and back a horse better than they,
Best would he be in all and best to us:
But how shall this be, with his cloistered ways?"
Then the King's heart was sore, for now the Prince
Begged sweet Yasôdhara for wife—in vain,
With Devadatta foremost at the bow,
Ardjuna master of all fiery steeds,
And Nanda chief in sword-play; but the Prince
Laughed low and said, "These things, too, I have learned;

Make proclamation that thy son will meet
All comers at their chosen games. I think
I shall not lose my love for such as these."
So 'twas given forth that on the seventh day
The Prince Siddârtha summoned whoso would
To match with him in feats of manliness,
The victor's crown to be Yasôdhara.

Therefore, upon the seventh day, there went
The Sâkya lords, and town and country round,
Unto the maidân ; and the maid went too
Amid her kinsfolk, carried as a bride,
With music, and with litters gaily dight,
And gold-horned oxen, flower-caparisoned :
Whom Devadatta claimed, of royal line,
And Nanda and Ardjuna, noble both,
The flower of all youths there ; till the Prince came
Riding his white horse Kantaka, which neighed,
Astonished at this great strange world without :
Also Siddârtha gazed with wondering eyes
On all those people born beneath the throne,
Otherwise housed than kings, otherwise fed,
And yet so like—perchance—in joys and griefs.
But when the Prince saw sweet Yasôdhara,
Brightly he smiled, and drew his silken rein,

Leaped to the earth from Kantaka's broad back,
And cried, "He is not worthy of this pearl
Who is not worthiest; let my rivals prove
If I have dared too much in seeking her."
Then Nanda challenged for the arrow-test
And set a brazen drum six gows away,
Ardjuna six and Devadatta eight;
But Prince Siddârtha bade them set his drum
Ten gows from off the line, until it seemed
A cowry-shell for target. Then they loosed,
And Nanda pierced his drum, Ardjuna his,
And Devadatta drove a well-aimed shaft
Through both sides of his mark, so that the crowd
Marvelled and cried; and sweet Yasôdhara
Dropped the gold sari o'er her fearful eyes,
Lest she should see her Prince's arrow fail.
But he, taking their bow of lacquered cane,
With sinews bound, and strung with silver wire,
Which none but stalwart arms could draw a span,
Thrummed it—low laughing—drew the twisted string
Till the horns kissed, and the thick belly snapped:
"That is for play, not love," he said; "hath none
A bow more fit for Sâkya lords to use?"
And one said, "There is Sinhahânu's bow,
Kept in the temple since we know not when,

Which none can string, nor draw if it be strung."
"Fetch me," he cried, "that weapon of a man!"
They brought the ancient bow, wrought of black steel,
Laid with gold tendrils on its branching curves
Like bison-horns; and twice Siddârtha tried
Its strength across his knee, then spake—"Shoot now
With this, my cousins!" but they could not bring
The stubborn arms a hand's-breadth nigher use;
Then the Prince, lightly leaning, bent the bow,
Slipped home the eye upon the notch, and twanged
Sharply the cord, which, like an eagle's wing
Thrilling the air, sang forth so clear and loud,
That feeble folk at home that day inquired
"What is this sound?" and people answered them,
"It is the sound of Sinhahânu's bow,
Which the King's son has strung and goes to shoot."
Then fitting fair a shaft, he drew and loosed,
And the keen arrow clove the sky, and drave
Right through that farthest drum, nor stayed its flight,
But skimmed the plain beyond, past reach of eye.

Next, Devadatta challenged with the sword,
And clove a Talas-tree six fingers thick;
Ardjuna seven; and Nanda cut through nine;
But two such stems together grew, and both

Siddârtha's blade shred at one flashing stroke,
Keen, but so smooth that the straight trunks upstood,
And Nanda cried, "His edge turned!" and the maid
Trembled anew seeing the trees erect;
Until the Devas of the air, who watched,
Blew light breaths from the south, and both green crowns
Crashed in the sand, clean-felled.

Then brought they steeds,
High-mettled, nobly-bred, and three times scoured
Around the maidân, but white Kantaka
Left even the fleetest far behind—so swift,
That ere the foam fell from his mouth to earth
Twenty spear-lengths he flew; but Nanda said,
"We too might win with such as Kantaka;
Fetch an unbroken horse, and let men see
Who best can back him." So the syces brought
A stallion dark as night, led by three chains,
Fierce-eyed, with nostrils wide and tossing mane,
Unshod, unsaddled, for no rider yet
Had crossed him. Three times each young Sâkya
Sprang to his mighty back, but the hot steed
Furiously reared, and flung them to the plain
In dust and shame; only Ardjuna held

His seat awhile ; and, bidding loose the chains,
Lashed the black flank, and shook the bit, and held
The proud jaws fast with grasp of master-hand,
So that in storms of wrath and rage and fear
The savage stallion circled once the plain
Half-tamed ; but sudden turned with naked teeth,
Gripped by the foot Ardjuna, tore him down,
And would have slain him, but the grooms ran in
Fettering the maddened beast. Then all men cried,
"Let not Siddârtha meddle with this Bhût,
Whose liver is a tempest, and his blood
Red flame ;" but the Prince said, "Let go the chains,
Give me his forelock only," which he held
With quiet grasp, and, speaking some low word,
Laid his right palm across the stallion's eyes,
And drew it gently down the angry face,
And all along the neck and panting flanks,
Till men astonished saw the night-black horse
Sink his fierce crest and stand subdued and meek,
As though he knew our Lord and worshipped him.
Nor stirred he while Siddârtha mounted ; then
Went soberly to touch of knee and rein
Before all eyes, so that the people said,
"Strive no more, for Siddârtha is the best."

And all the suitors answered "He is best!"
And Suprabuddha, father of the maid,
Said, "It was in our hearts to find thee best,
Being dearest, yet what magic taught thee more
Of manhood 'mid thy rose-bowers and thy dreams
Than war and chase and world's work bring to
these?
But wear, fair Prince, the treasure thou hast won."
Then at a word the lovely Indian girl
Rose from her place above the throng, and took
A crown of môgra-flowers, and lightly drew
The veil of black and gold across her brow,
Proud-pacing past the youths, until she came
To where Siddârtha stood in grace divine,
New lighted from the night-dark steed, which bent
Its strong neck meekly underneath his arm.
Before the Prince lowly she bowed, and bared
Her face celestial beaming with glad love;
Then on his neck she hung the fragrant wreath,
And on his breast she laid her perfect head,
And stooped to touch his feet with proud glad eyes,
Saying, "Dear Prince, behold me, who am thine!"
And all the throng rejoiced, seeing them pass
Hand fast in hand, and heart beating with heart,
The veil of black and gold drawn close again.

Long after—when enlightenment was come—
They prayed Lord Buddha touching all, and why
She wore this black and gold, and stepped so proud.
And the World-honoured answered, "Unto me
This was unknown, albeit it seemed half known;
For while the wheel of birth and death turns round,
Past things and thoughts, and buried lives come
back.
I now remember, myriad rains ago,
What time I roamed Himâla's hanging woods,
A tiger, with my striped and hungry kind;
I, who am Buddh, couched in the kusa grass
Gazing with green blinked eyes upon the herds
Which pastured near and nearer to their death
Round my day-lair; or underneath the stars
I roamed for prey, savage, insatiable,
Sniffing the paths for track of man and deer.
Amid the beasts that were my fellows then,
Met in deep jungle or by reedy jheel,
A tigress, comeliest of the forest, set
The males at war; her hide was lit with gold,
Black-broidered like the veil Yasôdhara
Wore for me; hot the strife waxed in that wood
With tooth and claw, while, underneath a neem
The fair beast watched us bleed, thus fiercely wooed.

And I remember, at the end she came,
Snarling, past this and that torn forest-lord
Whom I had conquered, and with fawning jaws
Licked my quick-heaving flank, and with me went
Into the wild with proud steps, amorously.
The wheel of birth and death turns low and high."

Therefore the maid was given unto the Prince
A willing spoil; and when the stars were good—
Mesha, the Red Ram, being Lord of heaven—
The marriage feast was kept, as Sâkyas use,
The golden gadi set, the carpet spread,
The wedding garlands hung, the arm-threads tied,
The sweet cake broke, the rice and attar thrown,
The two straws floated on the reddened milk,
Which, coming close, betokened "love till death;"
The seven steps taken thrice around the fire,
The gifts bestowed on holy men, the alms
And temple-offerings made, the mantras sung,
The garments of the bride and bridegroom tied.
Then the grey father spake: "Worshipful Prince,
She that was ours henceforth is only thine;
Be good to her, who hath her life in thee."
Wherewith they brought home sweet Yasôdhara,
With songs and trumpets, to the Prince's arms,

And love was all in all.

Yet not to love

Alone trusted the King; love's prison-house
Stately and beautiful he bade them build,
So that in all the earth no marvel was
Like Vishramvan, the Prince's pleasure-place.
Midway in those wide palace-grounds there rose
A verdant hill whose base Rohini bathed,
Murmuring adown from Himalay's broad feet,
To bear its tribute into Gunga's waves.
Southward a growth of tamarind trees and sâl,
Thick set with pale sky-coloured ganthi flowers,
Shut out the world, save if the city's hum
Came on the wind no harsher than when bees
Buzz out of sight in thickets. Northwards soared
The stainless ramps of huge Himâla's wall,
Ranged in white ranks against the blue—untrod,
Infinite, wonderful—whose uplands vast,
And lifted universe of crest and crag,
Shoulder and shelf, green slope and icy horn,
Riven ravine, and splintered precipice
Led climbing thought higher and higher, until
It seemed to stand in heaven and speak with gods.
Beneath the snows dark forests spread, sharp-laced
With leaping cataracts and veiled with clouds:

Lower grew rose-oaks and the great fir groves
Where echoed pheasant's call and panther's cry,
Clatter of wild sheep on the stones, and scream
Of circling eagles: under these the plain
Gleamed like a praying-carpet at the foot
Of those divinest altars. Fronting this
The builders set the bright pavilion up,
Fair-planted on the terraced hill, with towers
On either flank and pillared cloisters round.
Its beams were carved with stories of old time—
Radha and Krishna and the sylvan girls—
Sita and Hanuman and Draupadi;
And on the middle porch God Ganesha,
With disc and hook—to bring wisdom and wealth—
Propitious sate, wreathing his sidelong trunk.
By winding ways of garden and of court
The inner gate was reached, of marble wrought,
White, with pink veins; the lintel lazuli,
The threshold alabaster, and the doors
Sandal-wood, cut in pictured panelling;
Whereby to lofty halls and shadowy bowers
Passed the delighted foot, on stately stairs,
Through latticed galleries, 'neath painted roofs
And clustering columns, where cool fountains—fringed
With lotus and nelumbo—danced; and fish

Gleamed through their crystal, scarlet, gold, and blue.
Great-eyed gazelles in sunny alcoves browsed
The blown red roses ; birds of rainbow wing
Fluttered among the palms ; doves, green and grey,
Built their safe nests on gilded cornices ;
Over the shining pavements peacocks drew
The splendours of their trains, sedately watched
By milk-white herons and the small house-owls.
The plum-necked parrots swung from fruit to fruit ;
The yellow sunbirds whirred from bloom to bloom,
The timid lizards on the lattice basked
Fearless, the squirrels ran to feed from hand ;
For all was peace : the shy black snake, that gives
Fortune to households, sunned his sleepy coils
Under the moon-flowers, where the musk-deer played,
And brown-eyed monkeys chattered to the crows.
And all this House of love was peopled fair
With sweet attendance, so that in each part
With lovely sights were gentle faces found,
Soft speech and willing service ; each one glad
To gladden, pleased at pleasure, proud to obey ;
Till life glided beguiled, like a smooth stream
Banked by perpetual flow'rs, Yasôdhara
Queen of the enchanting Court.

But, innermost,

Beyond the richness of those hundred halls,
A secret chamber lurked, where skill had spent
All lovely fantasies to lull the mind.
The entrance of it was a cloistered square—
Roofed by the sky, and in the midst a tank—
Of milky marble built, and laid with slabs
Of milk-white marble ; bordered round the tank
And on the steps, and all along the frieze
With tender inlaid work of agate-stones.
Cool as to tread in summer-time on snows
It was to loiter there ; the sunbeams dropped
Their gold, and, passing into porch and niche,
Softened to shadows, silvery, pale, and dim,
As if the very Day paused and grew Eve
In love and silence at that bower's gate ;
For there beyond the gate the chamber was,
Beautiful, sweet ; a wonder of the world !
Soft light from perfumed lamps through windows fell,
Of nakre and stained stars of lucent film,
On golden cloths outspread, and silken beds,
And heavy splendour of the purdah's fringe,
Lifted to take only the loveliest in.
Here, whether it was night or day none knew,
For always streamed that softened light, more bright
Than sunrise, but as tender as the eve's ;

And always breathed sweet airs, more joy-giving
Than morning's, but as cool as midnight's breath;
And night and day lutes sighed, and night and day
Delicious foods were spread, and dewy fruits,
Sherbets new chilled with snows of Himalay,
And sweetmeats made of subtle daintiness,
With sweet tree-milk in its own ivory cup.
And night and day served there a chosen band
Of nautch girls, cup-bearers, and cymballers,
Delicate, dark-browed ministers of love,
Who fanned the sleeping eyes of the happy Prince,
And when he waked, led back his thoughts to bliss
With music whispering through the blooms, and charm
Of amorous songs and dreamy dances, linked
By chime of ankle-bells and wave of arms
And silver vina-strings; while essences
Of musk and champak, and the blue haze spread
From burning spices, soothed his soul again
To drowse by sweet Yasôdhara; and thus
Siddârtha lived forgetting.

Furthermore,

The King commanded that within those walls
No mention should be made of death or age,
Sorrow, or pain, or sickness. If one drooped
In the lovely Court—her dark glance dim, her feet

Faint in the dance—the guiltless criminal
Passed forth an exile from that Paradise,
Lest he should see and suffer at her woe.
Bright-eyed intendants watched to execute
Sentence on such as spake of the harsh world
Without, where aches and plagues were, tears and fears,

And wail of mourners, and grim fume of pyres.
'Twas treason if a thread of silver strayed
In tress of singing-girl or nautch-dancer;
And every dawn the dying rose was plucked,
The dead leaves hid, all evil sights removed:
For said the King, "If he shall pass his youth
Far from such things as move to wistfulness,

And brooding on the empty eggs of thought,
The shadow of this fate, too vast for man,
May fade, belike, and I shall see him grow
To that great stature of fair sovereignty
When he shall rule all lands—if he will rule—
The King of kings and Glory of his time."

Wherefore, around that pleasant prison-house—
Where love was gaoler and delights its bars—
But far removed from sight, the King bade build
A massive wall, and in the wall a gate
With brazen folding-doors, which but to roll
Back on their hinges asked a hundred arms;
Also the noise of that prodigious gate
Opening, was heard full half a yôjana.
And inside this another gate he made,
And yet within another—through the three
Must one pass if he quit that Pleasure-house.
Three mighty gates there were, bolted and barred,
And over each was set a faithful watch;
And the King's order said, "Suffer no man
To pass the gates, though he should be the Prince:
This on your lives—even though it be my son."

BOOK THE THIRD.

Book the Third.

IN which calm home of happy life and love
Ligged our Lord Buddha, knowing not of woe,
Nor want, nor pain, nor plague, nor age, nor death,
Save as when sleepers roam dim seas in dreams,
And land awearied on the shores of day,
Bringing strange merchandise from that black voyage.
Thus ofttimes, when he lay with gentle head
Lulled on the dark breasts of Yasôdhara,
Her fond hands fanning slow his sleeping lids,
He would start up and cry, "My world! Oh, world!
I hear! I know! I come!" And she would ask,
"What ails my Lord?" with large eyes terror-struck;
For at such times the pity in his look
Was awful, and his visage like a god's.

Then would he smile again to stay her tears,
And bid the vinas sound ; but once they set
A stringed gourd on the sill, there where the wind
Could linger o'er its notes and play at will—
Wild music makes the wind on silver strings—
And those who lay around heard only that ;
But Prince Siddârtha heard the Devas play,
And to his ears they sang such words as these :—

We are the voices of the wandering wind,
Which moan for rest, and rest can never find;
Lo! as the wind is, so is mortal life,
A moan, a sigh, a sob, a storm, a strife.

Wherefore and whence we are ye cannot know,
Nor where life springs, nor whither life doth go;
We are as ye are, ghosts from the inane,
What pleasure have we of our changeful pain?

What pleasure hast thou of thy changeless bliss?
Nay, if love lasted, there were joy in this;
But life's way is the wind's way, all these things
Are but brief voices breathed on shifting strings.

O Maya's son! because we roam he earth
Moan we upon these strings: we make no mirth,
So many woes we see in many lands,
So many streaming eyes and wringing hands.

Yet mock we while we wail, for, could they know,
This life they cling to is but empty show;
'Twere all as well to bid a cloud to stand,
Or hold a running river with the hand.

But thou that art to save, thine hour is nigh!
The sad world waiteth in its misery,
The blind world stumbleth on its round of pain;
Rise, Maya's child! wake! slumber not again!

We are the voices of the wandering wind:
Wander thou, too, O Prince, thy rest to find;
Leave love for love of lovers, for woe's sake
Quit state for sorrow, and deliverance make.

So sigh we, passing o'er the silver strings,
To thee who know'st not yet of earthly things;
So say we; mocking, as we pass away,
These lovely shadows wherewith thou dost play.

Thereafter it befel he sate at eve
Amid his beauteous Court, holding the hand
Of sweet Yasôdhara, and some maid told—
With breaks of music when her rich voice dropped—
An ancient tale to speed the hour of dusk,
Of love, and of a magic horse, and lands

Wonderful, distant, where pale peoples dwelled,
And where the sun at night sank into seas.
Then spake he, sighing, "Chitra brings me back
The wind's song in the strings with that fair tale:
Give her, Yasôdhara, thy pearl for thanks.
But thou, my pearl! is there so wide a world?

Is there a land which sees the great sun roll
Into the waves, and are their hearts like ours,
Countless, unknown, not happy—it may be—
Whom we might succour if we knew of them?
Ofttimes I marvel, as the Lord of day
Treads from the east his kingly road of gold,
Who first on the world's edge hath hailed his beam,
The children of the morning; oftentimes,
Even in thine arms and on thy breasts, bright wife,
Sore have I panted, at the sun's decline,
To pass with him into that crimson west
And see the peoples of the evening.
There must be many we should love—how else?
Now have I in this hour an ache, at last,
Thy soft lips cannot kiss away: oh, girl!
O Chitra! you that know of fairyland!
Where tether they that swift steed of thy tale?
My palace for one day upon his back,
To ride and ride and see the spread of the earth;
Nay, if I had yon callow vulture's plumes—
The carrion heir of wider realms than mine—
How would I stretch for topmost Himalay,
Light where the rose-gleam lingers on those snows,
And strain my gaze with searching what is round!

Why have I never seen and never sought?
Tell me what lies beyond our brazen gates."

Then one replied, "The city first, fair Prince!
The temples, and the gardens, and the groves,
And then the fields; and afterwards fresh fields,
With nullahs, maidâns, jungle, koss on koss;
And next King Bimbasâra's realm, and then
The vast flat world, with crores on crores of folk."
"Good," said Siddârtha; "let the word be sent
That Channa yoke my chariot—at noon
To-morrow I shall ride and see beyond."

Whereof they told the King: "Our Lord, thy son
Wills that his chariot be yoked at noon,
That he may ride abroad and see mankind."

"Yea!" spake the careful King, "'tis time he see;
But let the criers go about and bid
My city deck itself, so there be met
No noisome sight; and let none blind or maimed,
None that is sick, or stricken deep in years,
No leper, and no feeble folk come forth."
Therefore the stones were swept, and up and down
The water-carriers sprinkled all the streets

From spirting skins, the housewives scattered fresh
Red powder on their thresholds, strung new wreaths,
And trimmed the tulsi-bush before their doors.
The paintings on the walls were heightened up
With liberal brush, the trees set thick with flags,
The idols gilded ; in the four-went ways
Suryadeva and the great gods shone
'Mid shrines of leaves ; so that the city seemed
A capital of some enchanted land.
Also the criers passed, with drum and gong,
Proclaiming loudly, "Ho ! all citizens,
The King commands that there be seen to-day
No evil sight : let no one blind or maimed
None that is sick, or stricken deep in years,
No leper, and no feeble folk go forth.
Let none, too, burn his dead nor bring them out
'Till nightfall. Thus Suddhôdana commands."

So all was comely and the houses trim
Throughout Kapilavastu, while the Prince
Came forth in painted car, which two steers drew,
Snow-white, with swinging dewlaps, and huge humps
Wrinkled against the carved and lacquered yoke.
Goodly it was to mark the people's joy
Greeting their Prince ; and glad Siddârtha waxed

At sight of all those liege and friendly folk
Bright-clad and laughing as if life were good.
"Fair is the world," he said, "it likes me well!
And light and kind these men that are not kings,
And sweet my sisters here, who toil and tend;
What have I done for these to make them thus?
Why, if I love them, should those children know?
I pray take up yon pretty Sâkya boy
Who flung us flowers, and let him ride with me.
How good it is to reign in realms like this!
How simple pleasure is, if these be pleased
Because I come abroad! How many things
I need not if such little households hold
Enough to make our city full of smiles!
Drive, Channa! through the gates, and let me see
More of this gracious world I have not known."

So passed they through the gates, a joyous crowd
Thronging about the wheels, whereof some ran
Before the oxen, throwing wreaths; some stroked
Their silken flanks; some brought them rice and cakes,
All crying, "*Jai! jai!* for our noble Prince!"
Thus all the path was kept with gladsome looks
And filled with fair sights—for the King's word was
That such should be—when midway in the road,

Slow tottering from the hovel where he hid,
Crept forth a wretch in rags, haggard and foul,
An old, old man, whose shrivelled skin, sun-tanned,
Clung like a beast's hide to its fleshless bones.
Bent was his back with load of many days,
His eyepits red with rust of ancient tears,
His dim orbs blear with rheum, his toothless jaws
Wagging with palsy and the fright to see
So many and such joy. One skinny hand
Clutched a worn staff to prop his quavering limbs,
And one was pressed upon the ridge of ribs
Whence came in gasps the heavy painful breath.
"Alms!" moaned he, "give, good people! for I die
To-morrow or the next day!" then the cough
Choked him, but still he stretched his palm, and stood
Blinking, and groaning 'mid his spasms, "Alms!"
Then those around had wrenched his feeble feet
Aside, and thrust him from the road again,
Saying, "The Prince! dost see? get to thy lair!"
But that Siddârtha cried, "Let be! let be!
Channa! what thing is this who seems a man,
Yet surely only seems, being so bowed,
So miserable, so horrible, so sad?
Are men born sometimes thus? What meaneth he
Moaning 'to-morrow or next day I die?'

Finds he no food that so his bones jut forth?
What woe hath happened to this piteous one?"
Then answer made the charioteer, "Sweet Prince!
This is no other than an aged man;
Some fourscore years ago his back was straight,
His eye bright, and his body goodly: now
The thievish years have sucked his sap away,
Pillaged his strength and filched his will and wit;
His lamp has lost its oil, the wick burns black;
What life he keeps is one poor lingering spark
Which flickers for the finish: such is age;
Why should your Highness heed?" Then spake the
Prince:
"But shall this come to others, or to all,
Or is it rare that one should be as he?"
"Most noble," answered Channa, "even as he,
Will all these grow if they shall live so long."
"But," quoth the Prince, "if I shall live as long
Shall I be thus; and if Yasôdhara
Live fourscore years, is this old age for her,
Jâlîni, little Hasta, Gautami,
And Gunga, and the others?" "Yea, great Sir!"
The charioteer replied. Then spake the Prince:
"Turn back, and drive me to my house again!
I have seen that I did not think to see."

Which pondering, to his beauteous Court returned
Wistful Siddârtha, sad of mien and mood;
Nor tasted he the white cakes nor the fruits
Spread for the evening feast, nor once looked up
While the best palace-dancers strove to charm:
Nor spake—save one sad thing—when wofully
Yasôdhara sank to his feet and wept,
Sighing, "Hath not my Lord comfort in me?"
"Ah, Sweet!" he said, "such comfort that my soul
Aches, thinking it must end, for it will end,
And we shall both grow old, Yasôdhara!
Loveless, unlovely, weak, and old, and bowed.
Nay, though we locked up love and life with lips
So close that night and day our breaths grew one,
Time would thrust in between to filch away
My passion and thy grace, as black Night steals
The rose-gleams from yon peak, which fade to grey
And are not seen to fade. This have I found,
And all my heart is darkened with its dread,
And all my heart is fixed to think how Love
Might save its sweetness from the slayer, Time,
Who makes men old." So through that night he sate
Sleepless, uncomforted.

And all that night
The King Suddhôdana dreamed troublous dreams.

The first fear of his vision was a flag
Broad, glorious, glistening with a golden sun,
The mark of Indra ; but a strong wind blew,
Rending its folds divine, and dashing it
Into the dust ; whereat a concourse came
Of shadowy Ones, who took the spoiled silk up
And bore it eastward from the city gates.
The second fear was ten huge elephants,
With silver tusks and feet that shook the earth,
Trampling the southern road in mighty march ;
And he who sate upon the foremost beast
Was the King's son—the others followed him.
The third fear of the vision was a car,
Shining with blinding light, which four steeds drew,
Snorting white smoke and champing fiery foam ;
And in the car the Prince Siddârtha sate.
The fourth fear was a wheel which turned and turned,
With nave of burning gold and jewelled spokes,
And strange things written on the binding tire,
Which seemed both fire and music as it whirled.
The fifth fear was a mighty drum, set down
Midway between the city and the hills,
On which the Prince beat with an iron mace,
So that the sound pealed like a thunderstorm,
Rolling around the sky and far away.

The sixth fear was a tower, which rose and rose
High o'er the city till its stately head
Shone crowned with clouds, and on the top the Prince
Stood, scattering from both hands, this way and that,
Gems of most lovely light, as if it rained
Jacynths and rubies; and the whole world came,
Striving to seize those treasures as they fell
Towards the four quarters. But the seventh fear was
A noise of wailing, and behold six men
Who wept and gnashed their teeth, and laid their
palms
Upon their mouths, walking disconsolate.

These seven fears made the vision of his sleep,
But none of all his wisest dream-readers
Could tell their meaning. Then the King was wroth,
Saying, "There cometh evil to my house,
And none of ye have wit to help me know
What the great gods portend sending me this."
So in the city men went sorrowful
Because the King had dreamed seven signs of fear
Which none could read; but to the gate there came
An aged man, in robe of deer-skin clad,
By guise a hermit, known to none; he cried,
"Bring me before the King, for I can read

The vision of his sleep ;" who, when he heard
The sevenfold mysteries of the midnight dream,
Bowed reverent and said, "O Maharâj !
I hail this favoured House, whence shall arise
A wider-reaching splendour than the sun's !
Lo ! all these seven fears are seven joys,
Whereof the first, where thou didst see a flag—
Broad, glorious, gilt with Indra's badge—cast down
And carried out, did signify the end
Of old faiths and beginning of the new ;
For there is change with gods not less than men,
And as the days pass kalpas pass—at length.
The ten great elephants that shook the earth
The ten great gifts of wisdom signify,
In strength whereof the Prince shall quit his state
And shake the world with passage of the Truth.
The four flame-breathing horses of the car
Are those four fearless virtues which shall bring
Thy son from doubt and gloom to gladsome light ;
The wheel that turned with nave of burning gold
Was that most precious Wheel of perfect Law
Which he shall turn in sight of all the world.
The mighty drum whereon the Prince did beat,
Till the sound filled all lands, doth signify
The thunder of the preaching of the Word

Which he shall preach ; the tower that grew to heaven
The growing of the Gospel of this Buddh
Sets forth ; and those rare jewels scattered thence
The untold treasures are of that good Law
To gods and men dear and desirable.
Such is the interpretation of the tower ;
But for those six men weeping with shut mouths,
They are the six chief teachers whom thy son
Shall, with bright truth and speech unanswerable,
Convince of foolishness. O King ! rejoice ;
The fortune of my Lord the Prince is more
Than kingdoms, and his hermit-rags will be
Beyond fine cloths of gold. This was thy dream !
And in seven nights and days these things shall fall."
So spake the holy man, and lowly made
The eight prostrations, touching thrice the ground ;
Then turned and passed ; but when the King bade send
A rich gift after him, the messengers
Brought word, "We came to where he entered in
At Chandra's temple, but within was none
Save a grey owl which fluttered from the shrine."
The gods come sometimes thus.

But the sad King
Marvelled, and gave command that new delights
Be compassed to enthral Siddârtha's heart

Amid those dancers of his pleasure-house;
Also he set at all the brazen doors
A double guard.

Yet who shall shut out Fate?

For once again the spirit of the Prince
Was moved to see this world beyond his gates,
This life of man, so pleasant, if its waves
Ran not to waste and woful finishing
In Time's dry sands. "I pray you let me view
Our city as it is," such was his prayer
To King Suddhôdana. "Your Majesty
In tender heed hath warned the folk before
To put away ill things and common sights,
And make their faces glad to gladden me,
And all the causeways gay; yet have I learned
This is not daily life, and if I stand
Nearest, my father, to the realm and thee,
Fain would I know the people and the streets,
Their simple usual ways, and workday deeds,
And lives which those men live who are not kings.
Give me good leave, dear Lord! to pass unknown
Beyond my happy gardens; I shall come
The more contented to their peace again,

Or wiser, father, if not well content.
Therefore, I pray thee, let me go at will
To-morrow, with my servants, through the streets."
And the King said, amidst his Ministers,
"Belike this second flight may mend the first.
Note how the falcon starts at every sight
New from his hood, but what a quiet eye
Cometh of freedom; let my son see all,
And bid them bring me tidings of his mind."

Thus on the morrow, when the noon was come,
The Prince and Channa passed beyond the gates,
Which opened to the signet of the King;
Yet knew not they who rolled the great doors back
It was the King's son in that merchant's robe,
And in the clerkly dress his charioteer.
Forth fared they by the common way afoot,
Mingling with all the Sâkya citizens,
Seeing the glad and sad things of the town:
The painted streets alive with hum of noon,
The traders cross-legged 'mid their spice and grain,
The buyers with their money in the cloth,
The war of words to cheapen this or that,
The shout to clear the road, the huge stone wheels,
The strong slow oxen and their rustling loads,

The singing bearers with the palanquins,
The broad-necked hamals sweating in the sun,
The housewives bearing water from the well
With balanced chatties, and athwart their hips
The black-eyed babes; the fly-swarmed sweetmeat
shops,
The weaver at his loom, the cotton-bow
Twanging, the millstones grinding meal, the dogs
Prowling for orts, the skilful armourer
With tong and hammer linking shirts of mail,
The blacksmith with a mattock and a spear
Reddening together in his coals, the school
Where round their Guru, in a grave half-moon,
The Sâkya children sang the mantras through,
And learned the greater and the lesser gods;
The dyers stretching waistcloths in the sun
Wet from the vats—orange, and rose, and green;
The soldiers clanking past with swords and shields,
The camel-drivers rocking on the humps,
The Brahman proud, the martial Kshatriya,
The humble toiling Sudra; here a throng
Gathered to watch some chattering snake-tamer
Wind round his wrist the living jewellery
Of asp and nâg, or charm the hooded death
To angry dance with drone of beaded gourd;

There a long line of drums and horns, which went,
With steeds gay painted and silk canopies,
To bring the young bride home; and here a wife
Stealing with cakes and garlands to the god
To pray her husband's safe return from trade,
Or beg a boy next birth; hard by the booths
Where the swart potters beat the noisy brass
For lamps and lotas; thence, by temple walls
And gateways, to the river and the bridge
Under the city walls.
These had they passed
When from the roadside moaned a mournful voice,
"Help, masters! lift me to my feet; oh, help!
Or I shall die before I reach my house!"
A stricken wretch it was, whose quivering frame,
Caught by some deadly plague, lay in the dust
Writhing, with fiery purple blotches specked:
The chill sweat beaded on his brow, his mouth
Was dragged awry with twitchings of sore pain,
The wild eyes swam with inward agony.
Gasping, he clutched the grass to rise, and rose
Half-way, then sank, with quaking feeble limbs
And scream of terror, crying, "Ah, the pain!
Good people, help!" whereon Siddârtha ran,
Lifted the woful man with tender hands,

With sweet looks laid the sick head on his knee,
And, while his soft touch comforted the wretch,
Asked, "Brother, what is ill with thee? what harm
Hath fallen? wherefore can'st thou not arise?
Why is it, Channa, that he pants and moans,
And gasps to speak, and sighs so pitiful?"
Then spake the charioteer: "Great Prince! this man
Is smitten with some pest; his elements
Are all confounded; in his veins the blood,
Which ran a wholesome river, leaps and boils
A fiery flood; his heart, which kept good time,
Beats like an ill-played drum-skin, quick and slow;
His sinews slacken like a bowstring slipped;
The strength is gone from ham, and loin, and neck,
And all the grace and joy of manhood fled:
This is a sick man with the fit upon him.
See how he plucks and plucks to seize his grief,
And rolls his bloodshot orbs, and grinds his teeth,
And draws his breath as if 'twere choking smoke!
Lo! now he would be dead; but shall not die
Until the plague hath had its work in him,
Killing the nerves which die before the life;
Then, when his strings have cracked with agony
And all his bones are empty of the sense
To ache, the plague will quit and light elsewhere.

Oh, sir! it is not good to hold him so!
The harm may pass, and strike thee, even thee."
But spake the Prince, still comforting the man,
"And are there others, are there many thus?
Or might it be to me as now with him?"
"Great Lord!" answered the charioteer, "this comes
In many forms to all men; griefs and wounds,
Sickness and tetters, palsies, leprosies,
Hot fevers, watery wastings, issues, blains
Befall all flesh and enter everywhere."
"Come such ills unobserved?" the Prince inquired.
And Channa said, "Like the sly snake they come
That stings unseen; like the striped murderer,
Who waits to spring from the Karunda bush,
Hiding beside the jungle path; or like
The lightning, striking these and sparing those,
As chance may send."
"Then all men live in fear?"
"So live they, Prince!"
"And none can say, 'I sleep
Happy and whole to-night, and so shall wake?'"
"None say it."
"And the end of many aches,
Which come unseen, and will come when they come,
Is this, a broken body and sad mind,

And so old age?"
"Yea, if men last as long."
"But if they cannot bear their agonies,
Or if they will not bear, and seek a term;
Or if they bear, and be, as this man is,
Too weak except for groans, and so still live,
And growing old, grow older, then—what end?"
"They die, Prince."
"Die?"
"Yea, at the last comes Death,
In whatsoever way, whatever hour.
Some few grow old, most suffer and fall sick,
But all must die—behold, where comes the Dead!"

Then did Siddârtha raise his eyes, and see
Fast pacing towards the river-brink a band
Of wailing people; foremost one who swung
An earthen bowl with lighted coals; behind
The kinsmen, shorn, with mourning marks, ungirt,
Crying aloud, "O Rama, Rama, hear!
Call upon Rama, brothers;" next the bier,
Knit of four poles with bamboos interlaced,
Whereon lay—stark and stiff, feet foremost, lean,
Chapfallen, sightless, hollow-flanked, a-grin,
Sprinkled with red and yellow dust—the Dead,

Whom at the four-went ways they turned head first,
And crying "Rama, Rama!" carried on
To where a pile was reared beside the stream:
Thereon they laid him, building fuel up—
Good sleep hath one that slumbers on that bed!
He shall not wake for cold, albeit he lies
Naked to all the airs—for soon they set
The red flame to the corners four, which crept,
And licked, and flickered, finding out his flesh
And feeding on it with swift hissing tongues,
And crackle of parched skin, and snap of joint;
Till the fat smoke thinned and the ashes sank
Scarlet and grey, with here and there a bone
White midst the grey—the total of the man.

Then spake the Prince: "Is this the end which comes
To all who live?"
"This is the end that comes
To all," quoth Channa; "he upon the pyre—
Whose remnants are so petty that the crows
Caw hungrily, then quit the fruitless feast—
Ate, drank, laughed, loved, and lived, and liked life well.
Then came—who knows?—some gust of jungle wind,
A stumble on the path, a taint in the tank,
A snake's nip, half a span of angry steel,

A chill, a fishbone, or a falling tile,
And life was over and the man is dead.
No appetites, no pleasures, and no pains
Hath such; the kiss upon his lips is nought,
The fire-scorch nought; he smelleth not his flesh
A-roast, nor yet the sandal and the spice
They burn; the taste is emptied from his mouth,
The hearing of his ears is clogged, the sight
Is blinded in his eyes; those whom he loved
Wail desolate, for even that must go,
The body which was lamp unto the life,
Or worms will have a horrid feast of it.
Here is the common destiny of flesh:
The high and low, the good and bad, must die,
And then, 'tis taught, begin anew and live
Somewhere, somehow—who knows?—and so again
The pangs, the parting, and the lighted pile:—
Such is man's round."

But lo! Siddârtha turned
Eyes gleaming with divine tears to the sky,
Eyes lit with heavenly pity to the earth;
From sky to earth he looked, from earth to sky,
As if his spirit sought in lonely flight
Some far-off vision, linking this and that,
Lost—past—but searchable, but seen, but known.

Then cried he, while his lifted countenance
Glowed with the burning passion of a love
Unspeakable, the ardour of a hope
Boundless, insatiate : "Oh ! suffering world ;
Oh ! known and unknown of my common flesh,
Caught in this common net of death and woe,
And life which binds to both ! I see, I feel
The vastness of the agony of earth,
The vainness of its joys, the mockery
Of all its best, the anguish of its worst ;
Since pleasures end in pain, and youth in age,
And love in loss, and life in hateful death,
And death in unknown lives, which will but yoke
Men to their wheel again to whirl the round
Of false delights and woes that are not false.
Me too this lure hath cheated, so it seemed
Lovely to live, and life a sunlit stream
For ever flowing in a changeless peace ;
Whereas the foolish ripple of the flood
Dances so lightly down by bloom and lawn
Only to pour its crystal quicklier
Into the foul salt sea. The veil is rent
Which blinded me ! I am as all these men
Who cry upon their gods and are not heard,
Or are not heeded—yet there must be aid !

For them and me and all there must be help!
Perchance the gods have need of help themselves,
Being so feeble that when sad lips cry
They cannot save! I would not let one cry
Whom I could save How can it be that Brahm
Would make a world and keep it miserable,
Since, if, all-powerful, he leaves it so,
He is not good, and if not powerful,
He is not God?—Channa! lead home again!
It is enough! mine eyes have seen enough!"

Which when the King heard, at the gates he set
A triple guard; and bade no man should pass
By day or night, issuing or entering in,
Until the days were numbered of that dream.

BOOK THE FOURTH.

Book the Fourth.

BUT, when the days were numbered, then befell
The parting of our Lord—which was to be—
Whereby came wailing in the Golden Home,
Woe to the King and sorrow o'er the land,
But for all flesh deliverance, and that Law
Which whoso hears—the same shall make him free.

Softly the Indian night sinks on the plains
At full moon, in the month of Chaitra Shud,
When mangoes redden and the asôka buds
Sweeten the breeze, and Rama's birthday comes,
And all the fields are glad and all the towns.
Softly that night fell over Vishramvan,
Fragrant with blooms and jewelled thick with stars,

And cool with mountain airs sighing adown
From snow-flats on Himâla high outspread;
For the moon swung above the eastern peaks,
Climbing the spangled vault, and lighting clear
Rohini's ripples, and the hills and vales,
And all the sleeping land; and near at hand
Silvering those roof-tops of the pleasure-house,
Where nothing stirred nor sign of watching was,
Save at the outer gates, whose warders cried
Mudra, the watchword, and the countersign
Angana, and the watch-drums beat a round;
Whereat the earth lay still, except for yelp
Of prowling jackals, and the ceaseless trill
Of crickets in the garden grounds.
Within—
Where the moon glittered through the lace-worked stone,
Lighting the walls of pearl-shell and the floors
Paved with veined marble—softly fell her beams
On such rare company of Indian girls,
It seemed some chamber sweet in Paradise
Where Devîs rested. All the chosen ones
Of Prince Siddârtha's pleasure-home were there,
The brightest and most faithful of the Court;
Each form so lovely in the peace of sleep,

That you had said "This is the pearl of all!"
Save that beside her or beyond her lay
Fairer and fairer, till the pleasured gaze
Roamed o'er that feast of beauty as it roams
From gem to gem in some great goldsmith-work,
Caught by each colour till the next is seen.
With careless grace they lay, their soft brown limbs
Part hidden, part revealed; their glossy hair
Bound back with gold or flowers, or flowing loose
In black waves down the shapely nape and neck.
Lulled into pleasant dreams by happy toils,
They slept, no wearier than jewelled birds
Which sing and love all day, then under wing
Fold head, till morn bids sing and love again.
Lamps of chased silver swinging from the roof
In silver chains, and fed with perfumed oils,
Made with the moonbeams tender lights and shades,
Whereby were seen the perfect lines of grace,
The bosom's placid heave, the soft stained palms
Drooping or clasped, the faces fair and dark,
The great arched brows, the parted lips, the teeth
Like pearls a merchant picks to make a string,
The satin-lidded eyes, with lashes dropped
Sweeping the delicate cheeks, the rounded wrists,
The smooth small feet with bells and bangles decked,

Tinkling low music where some sleeper moved,
Breaking her smiling dream of some new dance
Praised by the Prince, some magic ring to find,
Some fairy love-gift. Here one lay full-length,
Her vina by her cheek, and in its strings
The little fingers still all interlaced
As when the last notes of her light song played
Those radiant eyes to sleep, and sealed her own.
Another slumbered folding in her arms
A desert-antelope, its slender head
Buried with black-sloped horns between her breasts,
Soft-nestling ; it was eating—when both drowsed—
Red roses, and her loosening hand still held
A rose half-mumbled, while a rose-leaf curled
Between the deer's lips. Here two friends had dozed
Together, weaving môgra-buds, which bound
Their sister-sweetness in a starry chain,
Linking them limb to limb and heart to heart,
One pillowed on the blossoms, one on her.
Another, ere she slept, was stringing stones
To make a necklet—agate, onyx, sard,
Coral, and moonstone—round her wrist it gleamed
A coil of splendid colour, while she held,
Unthreaded yet, the bead to close it up—
Green turkis, carved with golden gods and scripts.

Lulled by the cadence of the garden stream,
Thus lay they on the clustered carpets, each
A girlish rose with shut leaves, waiting dawn
To open and make daylight beautiful.
This was the ante-chamber of the Prince;
But at the purdah's fringe the sweetest slept—
Gunga and Gotami—chief ministers
In that still House of love.
The purdah hung,
Crimson and blue, with broidered threads of gold,
Across a portal carved in sandal-wood;
Whence by three steps the way was to the bower
Of inmost splendour, and the marriage-couch
Set on a dais soft with silver cloths,
Where the foot fell as though it trod on piles
Of neem-blooms. All the walls were plates of pearl,
Cut shapely from the shells of Lanka's wave;
And o'er the alabaster roof there ran
Rich inlayings of lotus and of bird,
Wrought in skilled work of lazulite and jade,
Jacynth and jasper; woven round the dome,
And down the sides, and all about the frames
Wherein were set the fretted lattices,
Through which there breathed, with moonlight and cool airs,

Scents from the shell-flowers and the jasmine sprays;
Not bringing thither grace or tenderness
Sweeter than shed from those fair presences
Within the place—the beauteous Sâkya Prince,
And hers, the stately, bright Yasôdhara.

Half risen from her soft nest at his side,
The chuddar fallen to her waist, her brow
Laid in both palms, the lovely Princess leaned
With heaving bosom and fast-falling tears.
Thrice with her lips she touched Siddârtha's hand,
And at the third kiss moaned, "Awake, my Lord!
Give me the comfort of thy speech!" Then he:
"What is it with thee, O my life?" but still
She moaned anew before the words would come;
Then spake, "Alas, my Prince! I sank to sleep
Most happy, for the babe I bear of thee
Quickened this eve, and at my heart there beat
That double pulse of life and joy and love
Whose happy music lulled me, but—aho!—
In slumber I beheld three sights of dread,
With thought whereof my heart is throbbing yet.
I saw a white bull with wide-branching horns,
A lord of pastures, pacing through the streets,
Bearing upon his front a gem which shone

As if some star had dropped to glitter there,
Or like the kantha-stone the great Snake keeps
To make bright daylight underneath the earth.
Slow through the streets towards the gates he paced,
And none could stay him, though there came a voice
From Indra's temple, 'If ye stay him not,
The glory of the city goeth forth.'
Yet none could stay him. Then I wept aloud,
And locked my arms about his neck, and strove,
And bade them bar the gates; but that ox-king
Bellowed, and, lightly tossing free his crest,
Broke from my clasp, and bursting through the bars,
Trampled the warders down and passed away.
The next strange dream was this: Four Presences
Splendid, with shining eyes, so beautiful
They seemed the Regents of the Earth who dwell
On Mount Sumeru, lighting from the sky
With retinue of countless heavenly ones,
Swift swept unto our city, where I saw
The golden flag of Indra on the gate
Flutter and fall; and lo! there rose instead
A glorious banner, all the folds whereof
Rippled with flashing fire of rubies sewn
Thick on the silver threads, the rays wherefrom
Set forth new words and weighty sentences

Whose message made all living creatures glad;
And from the east the wind of sunrise blew
With tender waft, opening those jewelled scrolls
So that all flesh might read; and wondrous blooms—
Plucked in what clime I know not—fell in showers,
Coloured as none are coloured in our groves."

Then spake the Prince: "All this, my Lotus-flower!
Was good to see."

"Ay, Lord," the Princess said,
"Save that it ended with a voice of fear
Crying, 'The time is nigh! the time is nigh!'
Thereat the third dream came; for when I sought
Thy side, sweet Lord! ah, on our bed there lay
An unpressed pillow and an empty robe—
Nothing of thee but those!—nothing of thee,
Who art my life and light, my king, my world!
And, sleeping still, I rose, and sleeping saw
Thy belt of pearls, tied here below my breasts,
Change to a stinging snake; my ankle-rings
Fall off, my golden bangles part and fall;
The jasmines in my hair wither to dust;
While this our bridal-couch sank to the ground,
And something rent the crimson purdah down:
Then far away I heard the white bull low,

And far away the embroidered banner flap,
And once again that cry, 'The time is come!'
But with that cry—which shakes my spirit still—
I woke! O Prince! what may such visions mean
Except I die, or—worse than any death—
Thou shouldst forsake me, or be taken?"
Soft
As the last smile of sunset was the look
Siddârtha bent upon his weeping wife.
"Comfort thee, dear!" he said, "if comfort lives
In changeless love! for though thy dreams may be
Shadows of things to come, and though the gods
Are shaken in their seats, and though the world
Stands nigh, perchance, to know some way of help,
Yet, whatsoever fall to thee and me,
Be sure I loved and love Yasôdhara.
Thou knowest how I muse these many moons,
Seeking to save the sad earth I have seen;
And when the time comes, that which will be will.
But if my soul yearns sore for souls unknown,
And if I grieve for griefs which are not mine,
Judge how my high-winged thoughts must hover here
O'er all these lives that share and sweeten mine—
So dear! and thine the dearest, gentlest, best,
And nearest. Ah, thou mother of my babe!

Whose body mixed with mine for this fair hope,
When most my spirit wanders, raging round
The lands and seas—as full of ruth for men
As the far-flying dove is full of ruth
For her twin nestlings—ever it has come
Home with glad wing and passionate plumes to thee,
Who art the sweetness of my kind best seen,
The utmost of their good, the tenderest
Of all their tenderness, mine most of all.
Therefore, whatever after this betide,
Bethink thee of that lordly bull which lowed,
That jewelled banner in thy dream which waved
Its folds departing, and of this be sure,
Always I loved and always love thee well,
And what I sought for all sought most for thee.
But thou, take comfort ; and, if sorrow falls,
Take comfort still in deeming there may be
A way to peace on earth by woes of ours ;
And have with this embrace what faithful love
Can think of thanks or frame for benison—
Too little, seeing love's strong self is weak—
Yet kiss me on the mouth, and drink these words
From heart to heart therewith, that thou mayst
know—
What others will not—that I loved thee most

Because I loved so well all living souls.
Now, Princess! rest; for I will rise and watch."

Then in her tears she slept, but sleeping sighed—
As if that vision passed again—"The time!
The time is come!" Whereat Siddârtha turned,
And, lo! the moon shone by the Crab! the stars
In that same silver order long foretold
Stood ranged to say, "This is the night!—choose thou
The way of greatness or the way of good:
To reign a King of kings, or wander lone,
Crownless and homeless, that the world be helped."
Moreover, with the whispers of the gloom,
Came to his ears again that warning song,
As when the Devas spoke upon the wind:
And surely Gods were round about the place
Watching our Lord, who watched the shining stars.

"I will depart," he spake; "the hour is come!
Thy tender lips, dear Sleeper, summon me
To that which saves the earth but sunders us;
And in the silence of yon sky I read
My fated message flashing. Unto this
Came I, and unto this all nights and days
Have led me; for I will not have that crown

Which may be mine: I lay aside those realms
Which wait the gleaming of my naked sword:
My chariot shall not roll with bloody wheels
From victory to victory, till earth
Wears the red record of my name. I choose
To tread its paths with patient, stainless feet,
Making its dust my bed, its loneliest wastes
My dwelling, and its meanest things my mates;
Clad in no prouder garb than outcasts wear,
Fed with no meats save what the charitable
Give of their will, sheltered by no more pomp
Than the dim cave lends or the jungle-bush.
This will I do because the woful cry
Of life and all flesh living cometh up
Into my ears, and all my soul is full
Of pity for the sickness of this world;
Which I will heal, if healing may be found
By uttermost renouncing and strong strife.
For which of all the great and lesser gods
Have power or pity? Who hath seen them—who?
What have they wrought to help their worshippers?
How hath it steaded man to pray, and pay
Tithes of the corn and oil, to chant the charms,
To slay the shrieking sacrifice, to rear
The stately fane, to feed the priests, and call

On Vishnu, Shiva, Surya, who save
None—not the worthiest—from the griefs that teach
Those litanies of flattery and fear
Ascending day by day, like wasted smoke?
Hath any of my brothers 'scaped thereby
The aches of life, the stings of love and loss,
The fiery fever and the ague-shake,
The slow, dull, sinking into withered age,
The horrible dark death—and what beyond
Waits—till the whirling wheel comes up again,
And new lives bring new sorrows to be borne,
New generations for the new desires
Which have their end in the old mockeries?
Hath any of my tender sisters found
Fruit of the fast or harvest of the hymn,
Or bought one pang the less at bearing-time
For white curds offered and trim tulsi-leaves?
Nay; it may be some of the Gods are good
And evil some, but all in action weak;
Both pitiful and pitiless, and both—
As men are—bound upon this wheel of change,
Knowing the former and the after lives.
For so our scriptures truly seem to teach,
That—once, and wheresoe'er, and whence begun—
Life runs its rounds of living, climbing up

From mote, and gnat, and worm, reptile, and fish,
Bird and shagged beast, man, demon, deva, God,
To clod and mote again ; so are we kin
To all that is ; and thus, if one might save
Man from his curse, the whole wide world should share
The lightened horror of this ignorance
Whose shadow is still fear, and cruelty
Its bitter pastime. Yea, if one might save !
And means must be ! There must be refuge ! Men
Perished in winter-winds till one smote fire
From flint-stones coldly hiding what they held,
The red spark treasured from the kindling sun.
They gorged on flesh like wolves, till one sowed corn,
Which grew a weed, yet makes the life of man ;
They mowed and babbled till some tongue struck speech,
And patient fingers framed the lettered sound.
What good gift have my brothers, but it came
From search and strife and loving sacrifice ?
If one, then, being great and fortunate,
Rich, dowered with health and ease, from birth designed
To rule—if he would rule—a King of kings ;
If one, not tired with life's long day but glad
I' the freshness of its morning, one not cloyed

With love's delicious feasts, but hungry still;
If one not worn and wrinkled, sadly sage,
But joyous in the glory and the grace
That mix with evils here, and free to choose
Earth's loveliest at his will: one even as I,
Who ache not, lack not, grieve not, save with griefs
Which are not mine, except as I am man;—
If such a one, having so much to give,
Gave all, laying it down for love of men,
And thenceforth spent himself to search for truth,
Wringing the secret of deliverance forth,
Whether it lurk in hells or hide in heavens,
Or hover, unrevealed, nigh unto all:
Surely at last, far off, sometime, somewhere,
The veil would lift for his deep-searching eyes,
The road would open for his painful feet,
That should be won for which he lost the world,
And Death might find him conqueror of death.
This will I do, who have a realm to lose,
Because I love my realm, because my heart
Beats with each throb of all the hearts that ache,
Known and unknown, these that are mine and those
Which shall be mine, a thousand million more
Saved by this sacrifice I offer now.
Oh, summoning stars! I come! Oh, mournful earth!

For thee and thine I lay aside my youth,
My throne, my joys, my golden days, my nights,
My happy palace—and thine arms, sweet Queen!
Harder to put aside than all the rest!
Yet thee, too, I shall save, saving this earth;
And that which stirs within thy tender womb,
My child, the hidden blossom of our loves,
Whom if I wait to bless my mind will fail.

Wife! child! father! and people! ye must share
A little while the anguish of this hour
That light may break and all flesh learn the Law.
Now am I fixed, and now I will depart,
Never to come again, till what I seek
Be found—if fervent search and strife avail."

So, with his brow he touched her feet, and bent

The farewell of fond eyes, unutterable,
Upon her sleeping face, still wet with tears;
And thrice around the bed in reverence,
As though it were an altar, softly stepped
With clasped hands laid upon his beating heart,
"For never," spake he, "lie I there again!"
And thrice he made to go, but thrice came back,
So strong her beauty was, so large his love:
Then, o'er his head drawing his cloth, he turned
And raised the purdah's edge:
There drooped, close-hushed,
In such sealed sleep as water-lilies know,
That lovely garden of his Indian girls;
The twin dark-petalled lotus-buds of all—
Gunga and Gotami—on either side,
And those, their silk-leaved sisterhood, beyond.
"Pleasant ye are to me, sweet friends!" he said,
"And dear to leave; yet, if I leave ye not,
What else will come to all of us save eld
Without assuage and death without avail?
Lo! as ye lie asleep so must ye lie
A-dead; and when the rose dies where are gone
Its scent and splendour? when the lamp is drained
Whither is fled the flame? Press heavy, Night!
Upon their down-dropped lids, and seal their lips,

That no tear stay me and no faithful voice.
For all the brighter that these made my life,
The bitterer it is that they and I,
And all, should live as trees do—so much spring,
Such and such rains and frosts, such winter-times,
And then dead leaves, with maybe spring again,
Or axe-stroke at the root. This will not I,
Whose life here was a God's !—this would not I,
Though all my days were godlike, while men moan
Under their darkness. Therefore farewell, friends!
While life is good to give, I give, and go
To seek deliverance and that unknown Light!"

Then, lightly treading where those sleepers lay,
Into the night Siddârtha passed: its eyes,
The watchful stars, looked love on him: its breath,
The wandering wind, kissed his robe's fluttered fringe;
The garden-blossoms, folded for the dawn,
Opened their velvet hearts to waft him scents
From pink and purple censers: o'er the land,
From Himalay unto the Indian Sea,
A tremor spread, as if earth's soul beneath
Stirred with an unknown hope; and holy books—
Which tell the story of our Lord say, too
That rich celestial musics thrilled the air

From hosts on hosts of shining ones, who thronged
Eastward and westward, making bright the night—
Northward and southward, making glad the ground.
Also those four dread Regents of the Earth,
Descending at the doorway, two by two,—
With their bright legions of Invisibles
In arms of sapphire, silver, gold, and pearl—
Watched with joined hands the Indian Prince, who
stood,
His tearful eyes raised to the stars, and lips
Close-set with purpose of prodigious love.

Then strode he forth into the gloom, and cried:
"Channa, awake! and bring out Kantaka!"
"What would my Lord?" the charioteer replied—
Slow-rising from his place beside the gate—
"To ride at night when all the ways are dark?"

"Speak low," Siddârtha said: "and bring my horse,
For now the hour is come when I should quit
This golden prison, where my heart lives caged,
To find the truth; which henceforth I will seek,
For all men's sake, until the truth be found."

"Alas! dear Prince," answered the charioteer,

"Spake then for nought those wise and holy men
Who cast the stars, and bade us wait the time
When King Suddhôdana's great son should rule
Realms upon realms, and be a Lord of lords?
Wilt thou ride hence and let the rich world slip
Out of thy grasp, to hold a beggar's bowl?
Wilt thou go forth into the friendless waste
That hast this Paradise of pleasures here?"

The Prince made answer, "Unto this I came,
And not for thrones: the kingdom that I crave
Is more than many realms—and all things pass
To change and death. Bring me forth Kantaka!"

"Most honoured," spake again the charioteer,
"Bethink thee of my Lord thy father's grief!
Bethink thee of their woe whose bliss thou art—
How shalt thou help them, first undoing them?"
Siddârtha answered, "Friend, that love is false
Which clings to love for selfish sweets of love;
But I, who love these more than joys of mine—
Yea, more than joy of theirs—depart to save
Them and all flesh, if utmost love avail:
Go, bring me Kantaka!"

Then Channa said,

"Master, I go!" and forthwith, mournfully,
Unto the stall he passed, and from the rack
Took down the silver bit and bridle-chains,
Breast-cord and curb, and knitted fast the straps,
And linked the hooks, and led out Kantaka:
Whom, tethering to the ring, he combed and dressed,
Stroking the snowy coat to silken gloss;
Next on the steed he laid the numdah square,
Fitted the saddle-cloth across, and set
The saddle fair, drew tight the jewelled girths,
Buckled the breech-bands and the martingale,
And made fall both the stirrups of worked gold.
Then over all he cast a golden net,
With tassels of seed-pearl and silken strings,
And led the great horse to the palace door,
Where stood the Prince; but when he saw his Lord,
Right glad he waxed and joyously he neighed,
Spreading his scarlet nostrils; and the books
Write, "Surely all had heard Kantaka's neigh,
And that strong trampling of his iron heels,
Save that the Devas laid soft unseen wings
Over their ears, and kept the sleepers deaf."

Fondly Siddârtha drew the proud head down,
Patted the shining neck, and said, "Be still,

White Kantaka! be still, and bear me now
The farthest journey ever rider rode;
For this night take I horse to find the truth,
And where my quest will end yet know I not,
Save that it shall not end until I find.
Therefore to-night, good steed, be fierce and bold!
Let nothing stay thee, though a thousand blades
Deny the road! let neither wall nor moat
Forbid our flight! Look! if I touch thy flank
And cry, 'On, Kantaka!' let whirlwinds lag
Behind thy course! Be fire and air, my horse!
To stead thy Lord; so shalt thou share with him
The greatness of this deed which helps the world;
For therefore ride I, not for men alone,
But for all things which, speechless, share our pain
And have no hope, nor wit to ask for hope.
Now, therefore, bear thy master valorously!"

Then to the saddle lightly leaping, he
Touched the arched crest, and Kantaka sprang forth
With armed hoofs sparkling on the stones, and ring
Of champing bit; but none did hear that sound,
For that the Suddha Devas, gathering near,
Plucked the red mohra-flowers and strewed them
thick

Under his tread, while hands invisible
Muffled the ringing bit and bridle-chains.
Moreover, it is written when they came
Upon the pavement near the inner gates,
The Yakshas of the air laid magic cloths
Under the stallion's feet, so that he went
Softly and still.

But when they reached the gate
Of tripled brass—which hardly fivescore men
Served to unbar and open—lo ! the doors
Rolled back all silently, though one might hear
In day-time two koss off the thunderous roar
Of those grim hinges and unwieldy plates.

Also the middle and the outer gates
Unfolded each their monstrous portals thus
In silence, as Siddârtha and his steed
Drew near ; while underneath their shadow lay,
Silent as dead men, all those chosen guards—
The lance and sword let fall, the shields unbraced,
Captains and soldiers—for there came a wind,
Drowsier than blows o'er Malwa's fields of sleep,
Before the Prince's path, which, being breathed,
Lulled every sense aswoon : and so he passed

Free from the palace.
When the morning star
Stood half a spear's length from the eastern rim,
And o'er the earth the breath of morning sighed,
Rippling Anoma's wave, the border-stream,
Then drew he rein, and leaped to earth, and kissed
White Kantaka betwixt the ears, and spake
Full sweet to Channa: "This which thou hast done
Shall bring thee good, and bring all creatures good:
Be sure I love thee always for thy love.
Lead back my horse, and take my crest-pearl here,
My princely robes, which henceforth stead me not,
My jewelled sword-belt and my sword, and these
The long locks by its bright edge severed thus
From off my brows. Give the King all, and say
Siddârtha prays forget him till he come
Ten times a Prince, with royal wisdom won
From lonely searchings and the strife for light;
Where, if I conquer, lo! all earth is mine—
Mine by chief service!—tell him—mine by love!
Since there is hope for man only in man,
And none hath sought for this as I will seek,
Who cast away my world to save my world."

BOOK THE FIFTH.

Book the Fifth.

ROUND Rajagriha five fair hills arose,
Guarding King Bimbisâra's sylvan town:
Baibhâra, green with lemon-grass and palms;
Bipulla, at whose foot thin Sarsuti
Steals with warm ripple; shadowy Tapovan,
Whose steaming pools mirror black rocks, which ooze
Sovereign earth-butter from their rugged roofs;
South-east the vulture-peak Sailâgiri;
And eastward Ratnagiri, hill of gems.
A winding track, paven with footworn slabs,
Leads thee, by safflower fields and bamboo tufts,
Under dark mangoes and the jujube-trees,
Past milk-white veins of rock and jasper crags,
Low cliff and flats of jungle-flowers, to where

The shoulder of that mountain, sloping west,
O'erhangs a cave with wild figs canopied.
Lo! thou who comest thither, bare thy feet
And bow thy head! for all this spacious earth
Hath not a spot more dear and hallowed. Here
Lord Buddha sate the scorching summers through,
The driving rains, the chilly dawns and eves;
Wearing for all men's sakes the yellow robe,
Eating in beggar's guise the scanty meal
Chance-gathered from the charitable; at night
Couched on the grass, homeless, alone; while yelped
The sleepless jackals round his cave, or coughs
Of famished tiger from the thicket broke.
By day and night here dwelt the World-honoured,
Subduing that fair body born for bliss
With fast and frequent watch and search intense
Of silent meditation, so prolonged
That ofttimes while he mused—as motionless
As the fixed rock his seat—the squirrel leaped
Upon his knee, the timid quail led forth
Her brood between his feet, and blue doves pecked
The rice-grains from the bowl beside his hand.

Thus would he muse from noontide—when the land
Shimmered with heat, and walls and temples danced

In the reeking air—till sunset, noting not
The blazing globe roll down, nor evening glide,
Purple and swift, across the softened fields;
Nor the still coming of the stars, nor throb
Of drum-skins in the busy town, nor screech
Of owl and night-jar; wholly wrapt from self
In keen unravelling of the threads of thought
And steadfast pacing of life's labyrinths.
Thus would he sit till midnight hushed the world,
Save where the beasts of darkness in the brake
Crept and cried out, as fear and hatred cry,
As lust and avarice and anger creep
In the black jungles of man's ignorance.
Then slept he for what space the fleet moon asks
To swim a tenth part of her cloudy sea;
But rose e'er the False-dawn, and stood again
Wistful on some dark platform of his hill,
Watching the sleeping earth with ardent eyes
And thoughts embracing all its living things;
While o'er the waving fields that murmur moved
Which is the kiss of Morn waking the lands,
And in the east that miracle of Day
Gathered and grew. At first a dusk so dim
Night seems still unaware of whispered dawn,
But soon—before the jungle-cock crows twice—

A white verge clear, a widening, brightening white,
High as the herald-star, which fades in floods
Of silver, warming into pale gold, caught
By topmost clouds, and flaming on their rims
To fervent golden glow, flushed from the brink
With saffron, scarlet, crimson, amethyst;
Whereat the sky burns splendid to the blue,
And, robed in raiment of glad light, the King
Of Life and Glory cometh!

Then our Lord,
After the manner of a Rishi, hailed
The rising orb, and went—ablutions made—
Down by the winding path unto the town;
And in the fashion of a Rishi passed
From street to street, with begging-bowl in hand,
Gathering the little pittance of his needs.
Soon was it filled, for all the townsmen cried,
"Take of our store, great sir!" and "Take of ours!"
Marking his godlike face and eyes enwrapt;
And mothers, when they saw our Lord go by,
Would bid their children fall to kiss his feet,
And lift his robe's hem to their brows, or run
To fill his jar, and fetch him milk and cakes.
And ofttimes as he paced, gentle and slow,
Radiant with heavenly pity, lost in care

For those he knew not, save as fellow-lives,
The dark surprised eyes of some Indian maid
Would dwell in sudden love and worship deep
On that majestic form, as if she saw
Her dreams of tenderest thought made true, and grace
Fairer than mortal fire her breast. But he
Passed onward with the bowl and yellow robe,
By mild speech paying all those gifts of hearts,
Wending his way back to the solitudes
To sit upon his hill with holy men,
And hear and ask of wisdom and its roads.

Midway on Ratnagiri's groves of calm,
Beyond the city, but below the caves,
Lodged such as hold the body foe to soul,
And flesh a beast which men must chain and tame
With bitter pains, till sense of pain is killed,
And tortured nerves vex torturer no more:
Yogis and Brahmacharis, Bhikshus, all
A gaunt and mournful band, dwelling apart.
Some day and night had stood with lifted arms,
Till—drained of blood and withered by disease—
Their slowly wasting joints and stiffened limbs
Jutted from sapless shoulders like dead forks

From forest trunks. Others had clenched their hands
So long and with so fierce a fortitude,
The claw-like nails grew through the festered palm.
Some walked on sandals spiked; some with sharp flints
Gashed breast and brow and thigh, scarred these with
fire,
Threaded their flesh with jungle thorns and spits,
Besmeared with mud and ashes, crouching foul
In rags of dead men wrapped about their loins.
Certain there were inhabited the spots
Where death-pyres smouldered, cowering defiled
With corpses for their company, and kites
Screaming around them o'er the funeral-spoils:
Certain who cried five hundred times a day
The names of Shiva, knit with hissing snakes
About their sun-tanned necks and hollow flanks,
One palsied foot drawn up against the ham.
So gathered they, a grievous company;
Crowns blistered by the blazing heat, eyes bleared,
Sinews and muscles shrivelled, visages
Haggard and wan as slain men's, five days dead;
Here crouched one in the dust who noon by noon
Meted a thousand grains of millet out,
Ate it with famished patience, seed by seed,
And so starved on; there one who bruised his pulse

With bitter leaves lest palate should be pleased ;
And next, a miserable saint self-maimed,
Eyeless and tongueless, sexless, crippled, deaf ;
The body by the mind being thus stripped
For glory of much suffering, and the bliss

Which they shall win—say holy books—whose woe
Shames gods that send us woe, and makes men gods
Stronger to suffer than Hell is to harm.

Whom sadly eyeing spake our Lord to one,
Chief of the woe-begones : " Much-suffering sir !

These many moons I dwell upon the hill—
Who am a seeker of the Truth—and see
My brothers here, and thee, so piteously
Self-anguished ; wherefore add ye ills to life
Which is so evil ?"
Answer made the sage :
"'Tis written if a man shall mortify
His flesh, till pain be grown the life he lives
And death voluptuous rest, such woes shall purge
Sin's dross away, and the soul, purified,
Soar from the furnace of its sorrow, winged
For glorious spheres and splendour past all thought."

"Yon cloud which floats in heaven," the Prince replied,
"Wreathed like gold cloth around your Indra's throne,
Rose thither from the tempest-driven sea ;
But it must fall again in tearful drops,
Trickling through rough and painful water-ways
By cleft and nullah and the muddy flood,
To Gunga and the sea, wherefrom it sprang.
Know'st thou, my brother, if it be not thus,
After their many pains, with saints in bliss ?
Since that which rises falls, and that which buys
Is spent ; and if ye buy heav'n with your blood

In hell's hard market, when the bargain's through
The toil begins again!"
"It may begin,"
The hermit moaned. "Alas! we know not this,
Nor surely anything; yet after night
Day comes, and after turmoil peace, and we
Hate this accursed flesh which clogs the soul
That fain would rise; so, for the sake of soul,
We stake brief agonies in game with Gods
To gain the larger joys."
"Yet if they last
A myriad years," he said, "they fade at length,
Those joys; or if not, is there then some life
Below, above, beyond, so unlike life
It will not change? Speak! do your Gods endure
For ever, brothers?"
"Nay," the Yogis said,
"Only great Brahm endures: the Gods but live."

Then spake Lord Buddha: "Will ye, being wise,
As ye seem holy and strong-hearted ones,
Throw these sore dice, which are your groans and moans,
For gains which may be dreams, and must have end?
Will ye, for love of soul, so loathe your flesh,

So scourge and maim it, that it shall not serve
To bear the spirit on, searching for home,
But founder on the track before night-fall,
Like willing steed o'er-spurred? Will ye, sad sirs!
Dismantle and dismember this fair house,
Where we have come to dwell by painful pasts;
Whose windows give us light—the little light—
Whereby we gaze abroad to know if dawn
Will break, and whither winds the better road?"

Then cried they, "We have chosen this for road
And tread it, Rajaputra! till the close—
Though all its stones were fire—in trust of death.
Speak, if thou know'st a way more excellent;
If not, peace go with thee!"

Onward he passed,
Exceeding sorrowful, seeing how men
Fear so to die they are afraid to fear,
Lust so to live they dare not love their life,
But plague it with fierce penances, belike
To please the Gods who grudge pleasure to man;
Belike to baulk hell by self-kindled hells;
Belike in holy madness, hoping soul
May break the better through their wasted flesh.
"Oh, flowerets of the field!" Siddârtha said,

"Who turn your tender faces to the sun—
Glad of the light, and grateful with sweet breath
Of fragrance and these robes of reverence donned
Silver and gold and purple—none of ye
Miss perfect living, none of ye despoil
Your happy beauty. Oh, ye palms! which rise
Eager to pierce the sky and drink the wind
Blown from Malaya and the cool blue seas,
What secret know ye that ye grow content,
From time of tender shoot to time of fruit,
Murmuring such sun-songs from your feathered crowns?
Ye, too, who dwell so merry in the trees—
Quick-darting parrots, bee-birds, bulbuls, doves—
None of ye hate your life, none of ye deem
To strain to better by foregoing needs!
But man, who slays ye—being lord—is wise,
And wisdom, nursed on blood, cometh thus forth
In self-tormentings!"
While the Master spake
Blew down the mount the dust of pattering feet,
White goats and black sheep winding slow their way,
With many a lingering nibble at the tufts,
And wanderings from the path, where water gleamed
Or wild figs hung. But always as they strayed
The herdsman cried, or slung his sling, and kept

The silly crowd still moving to the plain.
A ewe with couplets in the flock there was,
Some hurt had lamed one lamb, which toiled behind
Bleeding, while in the front its fellow skipped,
And the vexed dam hither and thither ran,
Fearful to lose this little one or that;
Which when our Lord did mark, full tenderly
He took the limping lamb upon his neck,
Saying, "Poor woolly mother, be at peace!
Whither thou goest I will bear thy care;
Twere all as good to ease one beast of grief
As sit and watch the sorrows of the world
In yonder caverns with the priests who pray."

"But," spake he to the herdsmen, "wherefore, friends!
Drive ye the flocks adown under high noon,
Since 'tis at evening that men fold their sheep?"
And answer gave the peasants: "We are sent
To fetch a sacrifice of goats five-score,
And five-score sheep, the which our Lord the King
Slayeth this night in worship of his gods."
Then said the Master: "I will also go!"
So paced he patiently, bearing the lamb

Beside the herdsmen in the dust and sun,
The wistful ewe low bleating at his feet.

Whom, when they came unto the river-side
A woman—dove-eyed, young, with tearful face
And lifted hands—saluted, bending low:

"Lord! thou art he," she said, "who yesterday
Had pity on me in the fig-grove here,
Where I live lone and reared my child; but he
Straying amid the blossoms found a snake,
Which twined about his wrist, whilst he did laugh

And tease the quick-forked tongue and opened mouth
Of that cold playmate. But, alas! ere long
He turned so pale and still, I could not think
Why he should cease to play, and let my breast
Fall from his lips. And one said, 'He is sick
Of poison;' and another, 'He will die.'
But I, who could not lose my precious boy,
Prayed of them physic, which might bring the light
Back to his eyes; it was so very small,
That kiss-mark of the serpent, and I think
It could not hate him, gracious as he was,
Nor hurt him in his sport. And some one said,
'There is a holy man upon the hill—
Lo! now he passeth in the yellow robe—
Ask of the Rishi if there be a cure
For that which ails thy son.' Whereon I came
Trembling to thee, whose brow is like a god's,
And wept and drew the face-cloth from my babe,
Praying thee tell what simples might be good.
And thou, great sir! didst spurn me not, but gaze
With gentle eyes and touch with patient hand;
Then draw the face-cloth back, saying to me,
'Yea! little sister, there is that might heal
Thee first, and him, if thou couldst fetch the thing;

For they who seek physicians bring to them
What is ordained. Therefore, I pray thee, find
Black mustard-seed, a tola ; only mark
Thou take it not from any hand or house

Where father, mother, child, or slave hath died :
It shall be well if thou canst find such seed.'
Thus didst thou speak, my Lord !"
The Master smiled
Exceeding tenderly. "Yea ! I spake thus,

Dear Kisagôtami! But didst thou find
The seed?"
"I went, Lord, clasping to my breast
The babe, grown colder, asking at each hut—
Here in the jungle and towards the town—
'I pray you, give me mustard, of your grace,
A tola—black;' and each who had it gave,
For all the poor are piteous to the poor;
But when I asked, 'In my friend's household here
Hath any peradventure ever died—
Husband, or wife, or child, or slave?' they said:
'O Sister! what is this you ask? the dead
Are very many, and the living few!'
So with sad thanks I gave the mustard back,
And prayed of others; but the others said,
'Here is the seed, but we have lost our slave!'
'Here is the seed, but our good man is dead!'
'Here is some seed, but he that sowed it died
Between the rain-time and the harvesting!'
Ah, sir! I could not find a single house
Where there was mustard-seed and none had died!
Therefore I left my child—who would not suck
Nor smile—beneath the wild-vines by the stream,
To seek thy face and kiss thy feet, and pray
Where I might find this seed and find no death,

If now, indeed, my baby be not dead,
As I do fear, and as they said to me."

"My sister! thou hast found," the Master said,
"Searching for what none finds—that bitter balm
I had to give thee. He thou lovedst slept
Dead on thy bosom yesterday: to-day
Thou know'st the whole wide world weeps with thy woe:
The grief which all hearts share grows less for one.
Lo! I would pour my blood if it could stay
Thy tears and win the secret of that curse
Which makes sweet love our anguish, and which drives—
O'er flowers and pastures to the sacrifice—
As these dumb beasts are driven—men their lords.
I seek that secret: bury thou thy child!"

So entered they the city side by side,
The herdsmen and the Prince, what time the sun
Gilded slow Sona's distant stream, and threw
Long shadows down the street and through the gate
Where the King's men kept watch. But when these saw
Our Lord bearing the lamb, the guards stood back,
The market-people drew their wains aside,
In the bazaar buyers and sellers stayed

The war of tongues to gaze on that mild face;
The smith, with lifted hammer in his hand,
Forgot to strike; the weaver left his web,
The scribe his scroll, the money-changer lost
His count of cowries; from the unwatched rice
Shiva's white bull fed free; the wasted milk
Ran o'er the lota while the milkers watched
The passage of our Lord moving so meek,
With yet so beautiful a majesty.
But most the women gathering in the doors
Asked, "Who is this that brings the sacrifice
So graceful and peace-giving as he goes?
What is his caste? whence hath he eyes so sweet?
Can he be Sâkra or the Devaraj?"
And others said, "It is the holy man
Who dwelleth with the Rishis on the hill."
But the Lord paced, in meditation lost,
Thinking, "Alas! for all my sheep which have
No shepherd; wandering in the night with none
To guide them; bleating blindly towards the knife
Of Death, as these dumb beasts which are their kin."

Then some one told the King, "There cometh here
A holy hermit, bringing down the flock
Which thou didst bid to crown thy sacrifice."

The King stood in his hall of offering,
On either hand the white-robed Brahmans ranged
Muttered their mantras, feeding still the fire
Which roared upon the midmost altar. There
From scented woods flickered bright tongues of flame,
Hissing and curling as they licked the gifts
Of ghee and spices and the Soma juice,
The joy of Indra. Round about the pile
A slow, thick, scarlet streamlet smoked and ran,
Sucked by the sand, but ever rolling down,
The blood of bleating victims. One such lay,
A spotted goat, long-horned, its head bound back
With munja grass; at its stretched throat the knife
Pressed by a priest, who murmured, "This, dread gods,
Of many yajnas cometh as the crown
From Bimbisâra: take ye joy to see
The spirted blood, and pleasure in the scent
Of rich flesh roasting 'mid the fragrant flames;
Let the King's sins be laid upon this goat,
And let the fire consume them burning it,
For now I strike."
But Buddha softly said,
"Let him not strike, great King!" and therewith loosed
The victim's bonds, none staying him, so great

His presence was. Then, craving leave, he spake
Of life, which all can take but none can give,
Life, which all creatures love and strive to keep,
Wonderful, dear, and pleasant unto each,
Even to the meanest ; yea, a boon to all
Where pity is; for pity makes the world
Soft to the weak and noble for the strong.
Unto the dumb lips of his flock he lent
Sad pleading words, showing how man, who prays
For mercy to the gods, is merciless,
Being as god to those ; albeit all life
Is linked and kin, and what we slay have given
Meek tribute of the milk and wool, and set
Fast trust upon the hands which murder them.
Also he spake of what the holy books
Do surely teach, how that at death some sink
To bird and beast, and these rise up to man
In wanderings of the spark which grows purged flame.
So were the sacrifice new sin, if so
The fated passage of a soul be stayed.
Nor, spake he, shall one wash his spirit clean
By blood ; nor gladden gods, being good, with blood ;
Nor bribe them, being evil ; nay, nor lay
Upon the brow of innocent bound beasts
One hair's weight of that answer all must give

For all things done amiss or wrongfully,
Alone, each for himself, reckoning with that
The fixed arithmic of the universe,
Which meteth good for good and ill for ill,
Measure for measure, unto deeds, words, thoughts ;
Watchful, aware, implacable, unmoved ;
Making all futures fruits of all the pasts.
Thus spake he, breathing words so piteous,
With such high lordliness of ruth and right,
The priests drew down their garments o'er the hands
Crimsoned with slaughter, and the King came near,
Standing with clasped palms reverencing Buddh ;
While still our Lord went on, teaching how fair
This earth were if all living things be linked
In friendliness and common use of foods,
Bloodless and pure ; the golden grain, bright fruits,
Sweet herbs which grow for all, the waters wan,
Sufficient drinks and meats. Which when these heard,
The might of gentleness so conquered them,
The priests themselves scattered their altar-flames
And flung away the steel of sacrifice ;
And through the land next day passed a decree
Proclaimed by criers, and in this wise graved
On rock and column : "Thus the King's will is :—
There hath been slaughter for the sacrifice

And slaying for the meat, but henceforth none
Shall spill the blood of life nor taste of flesh,
Seeing that knowledge grows, and life is one,
And mercy cometh to the merciful."
So ran the edict, and from those days forth
Sweet peace hath spread between all living kind,
Man and the beasts which serve him, and the birds,
On all those banks of Gunga where our Lord
Taught with his saintly pity and soft speech.

For aye so piteous was the Master's heart
To all that breathe this breath of fleeting life,
Yoked in one fellowship of joys and pains,
That it is written in the holy books
How, in an ancient age—when Buddha wore
A Brahman's form, dwelling upon the rock
Named Munda, by the village of Dâlidd—
Drought withered all the land : the young rice died
Ere it could hide a quail ; in forest glades
A fierce sun sucked the pools ; grasses and herbs
Sickened, and all the woodland creatures fled
Scattering for sustenance. At such a time,
Between the hot walls of a nullah, stretched
On naked stones, our Lord spied, as he passed,
A starving tigress. Hunger in her orbs

Glared with green flame ; her dry tongue lolled a span
Beyond the gasping jaws and shrivelled jowl :
Her painted hide hung wrinkled on her ribs,
As when between the rafters sinks a thatch
Rotten with rains ; and at the poor lean dugs
Two cubs, whining with famine, tugged and sucked,
Mumbling those milkless teats which rendered nought ;
While she, their gaunt dam, licked full motherly
The clamorous twins, and gave her flank to them
With moaning throat, and love stronger than want,
Softening the first of that wild cry wherewith
She laid her famished muzzle to the sand
And roared a savage thunder-peal of woe.
Seeing which bitter strait, and heeding nought
Save the immense compassion of a Buddh,
Our Lord bethought : "There is no other way
To help this murderess of the woods but one.
By sunset these will die, having no meat :
There is no living heart will pity her,
Bloody with ravin, lean for lack of blood.
Lo ! if I feed her, who shall lose but I,
And how can love lose doing of its kind
Even to the uttermost ?" So saying, Buddh
Silently laid aside sandals and staff,
His sacred thread, turban, and cloth, and came

Forth from behind the milk-bush on the sand,
Saying, "Ho! mother, here is meat for thee!"
Whereat the perishing beast yelped hoarse and shrill,
Sprang from her cubs, and, hurling to the earth
That willing victim, had her feast of him
With all the crooked daggers of her claws
Rending his flesh, and all her yellow fangs
Bathed in his blood: the great cat's burning breath
Mixed with the last sigh of such fearless love.

Thus large the Master's heart was long ago,
Not only now, when with his gracious ruth
He bade cease cruel worship of the Gods.
And much King Bimbisâra prayed our Lord—
Learning his royal birth and holy search—
To tarry in that city, saying oft,
"Thy princely state may not abide such fasts;
Thy hands were made for sceptres, not for alms.
Sojourn with me, who have no son to rule,
And teach my kingdom wisdom, till I die,
Lodged in my palace with a beauteous bride."
But ever spake Siddârtha, of set mind:
"These things I had, most noble King, and left,
Seeking the truth; which still I seek, and shall;
Not to be stayed though Sâkra's palace ope'd

Its doors of pearl and Devîs wooed me in.
I go to build the Kingdom of the Law,
Journeying to Gaya and the forest shades,
Where, as I think, the light will come to me;
For nowise here among the Rishis comes
That light, nor from the Shasters, nor from fasts
Borne till the body faints, starved by the soul.
Yet there is light to reach and truth to win;
And surely, O true Friend, if I attain
I will return and quit thy love."

Thereat

Thrice round the Prince King Bimbisâra paced,
Reverently bending to the Master's feet,
And bade him speed. So passed our Lord away
Towards Uravilva, not yet comforted,
And wan of face, and weak with six years' quest.
But they upon the hill and in the grove—
Alâra, Udra, and the ascetics five—
Had stayed him, saying all was written clear
In holy Shasters, and that none might win
Higher than *Sruti* and than *Smriti*—nay,
Not the chief saints!—for how should mortal man
Be wiser than the Jnana-Kând, which tells
That Brahm is bodiless and actionless,
Passionless, calm, unqualified, unchanged,

Pure life, pure thought, pure joy? Or how should man
Be better than the Karmma-Kând, which shows
How he may strip passion and action off,
Break from the bond of self, and so, unsphered,
Be God, and melt into the vast divine;
Flying from false to true, from wars of sense
To peace eternal, where the Silence lives?

But the Prince heard them, not yet comforted.

BOOK THE SIXTH

Book the Sixth.

THOU, who wouldst see where
dawned the light at last,
North-westwards from the
"Thousand Gardens" go
By Gunga's valley till thy steps
be set
On the green hills where those
twin streamlets spring,
Nilâjan and Mohâna ; follow them,
Winding beneath broad-leaved mahûa-trees,
'Mid thickets of the sansâr and the bir,
Till on the plain the shining sisters meet
In Phalgu's bed, flowing by rocky banks
To Gâya and the red Barabar hills.
Hard by that river spreads a thorny waste,
Uruwelaya named in ancient days,
With sandhills broken ; on its verge a wood
Waves sea-green plumes and tassels thwart the sky,

With undergrowth wherethrough a still flood steals,
Dappled with lotus-blossoms, blue and white,
And peopled with quick fish and tortoises.
Near it the village of Senâni reared
Its roofs of grass, nestled amid the palms,
Peaceful with simple folk and pastoral toils.

There in the sylvan solitudes once more
Lord Buddha lived, musing the woes of men,
The ways of fate, the doctrines of the books,
The lessons of the creatures of the brake,
The secrets of the silence whence all come,
The secrets of the gloom whereto all go,
The life which lies between, like that arch flung
From cloud to cloud across the sky, which hath
Mists for its masonry and vapoury piers,
Melting to void again which was so fair
With sapphire hues, garnet, and chrysoprase.
Moon after moon our Lord sate in the wood,
So meditating these that he forgot
Ofttimes the hour of food, rising from thoughts
Prolonged beyond the sunrise and the noon,
To see his bowl unfilled, and eat perforce
Of wild fruit fallen from the boughs o'erhead,
Shaken to earth by chattering ape or plucked

By purple parokeet. Therefore his grace
Faded; his body, worn by stress of soul,
Lost day by day the marks, thirty and two,
Which testify the Buddha. Scarce that leaf,
Fluttering so dry and withered to his feet
From off the sâl-branch, bore less likeliness
Of spring's soft greenery than he of him
Who was the princely flower of all his land.

And once, at such a time, the o'erwrought Prince
Fell to the earth in deadly swoon, all spent,
Even as one slain, who hath no longer breath
Nor any stir of blood; so wan he was,
So motionless. But there came by that way
A shepherd-boy, who saw Siddârtha lie
With lids fast-closed, and lines of nameless pain
Fixed on his lips—the fiery noonday sun
Beating upon his head—who, plucking boughs
From wild rose-apple trees, knitted them thick
Into a bower to shade the sacred face.
Also he poured upon the Master's lips
Drops of warm milk, pressed from his she-goat's bag,
Lest, being low caste, he, by touching, wrong one
So high and holy seeming. But the books
Tell how the jambu-branches, planted thus,

Shot with quick life, in wealth of leaf and flower,
And glowing fruitage interlaced and close,
So that the bower grew like a tent of silk
Pitched for a king at hunting, decked with studs
Of silver-work and bosses of red gold.
And the boy worshipped, deeming him some God;
But our Lord gaining breath, arose and asked
Milk in the shepherd's lota. "Ah, my Lord,
I cannot give thee," quoth the lad; "thou seest
I am a Sudra, and my touch defiles!"
Then the World-honoured spake: "Pity and need
Make all flesh kin. There is no caste in blood,
Which runneth of one hue, nor caste in tears,
Which trickle salt with all; neither comes man
To birth with tilka-mark stamped on the brow,
Nor sacred thread on neck. Who doth right deed
Is twice-born, and who doeth ill deeds vile.
Give me to drink, my brother; when I come
Unto my quest it shall be good for thee."
Thereat the peasant's heart was glad, and gave

And on another day there passed that road
A band of tinselled girls, the nautch-dancers
Of Indra's temple in the town, with those
Who made their music—one that beat a drum

Set round with peacock-feathers, one that blew
The piping bánsuli, and one that twitched
A three-string sitar. Lightly tripped they down
From ledge to ledge and through the chequered paths
To some gay festival, the silver bells
Chiming soft peals about the small brown feet,
Armlets and wrist-rings tattling answer shrill;
While he that bore the sitar thrummed and twanged
His threads of brass, and she beside him sang—

"Fair goes the dancing when the sitar's tuned;
Tune us the sitar neither low nor high,
And we will dance away the hearts of men.

The string o'erstretched breaks, and the music flies;
The string o'erslack is dumb, and music dies;
Tune us the sitar neither low nor high."

So sang the nautch-girl to the pipe and wires,
Fluttering like some vain, painted butterfly
From glade to glade along the forest path,
Nor dreamed her light words echoed on the ear
Of him, that holy man, who sate so rapt
Under the fig-tree by the path. But Buddh
Lifted his great brow as the wantons passed,

And spake: "The foolish ofttimes teach the wise;
I strain too much this string of life, belike,
Meaning to make such music as shall save.
Mine eyes are dim now that they see the truth,
My strength is waned now that my need is most;
Would that I had such help as man must have,
For I shall die, whose life was all men's hope."

Now, by that river dwelt a landholder
Pious and rich, master of many herds,
A goodly chief, the friend of all the poor;
And from his house the village drew its name—
"Senâni." Pleasant and in peace he lived,
Having for wife Sujâta, loveliest
Of all the dark-eyed daughters of the plain;
Gentle and true, simple and kind was she,
Noble of mien, with gracious speech to all
And gladsome looks—a pearl of womanhood
Passing calm years of household happiness
Beside her lord in that still Indian home,
Save that no male child blessed their wedded love.
Wherefore, with many prayers she had besought
Lukshmi; and many nights at full-moon gone
Round the great Lingam, nine times nine, with gifts
Of rice and jasmine wreaths and sandal oil

Praying a boy ; also Sujâta vowed—
If this should be—an offering of food
Unto the Wood-God, plenteous, delicate,
Set in a bowl of gold under his tree,
Such as the lips of Devs may taste and take.
And this had been : for there was born to her
A beauteous boy, now three months old, who lay
Between Sujâta's breasts, while she did pace
With grateful footsteps to the Wood-God's shrine,
One arm clasping her crimson sari close
To wrap the babe, that jewel of her joys,
The other lifted high in comely curve
To steady on her head the bowl and dish
Which held the dainty victuals for the God.

But Radha, sent before to sweep the ground
And tie the scarlet threads around the tree,
Came eager, crying, "Ah, dear Mistress ! look.
There is the Wood-God sitting in his place,
Revealed, with folded hands upon his knees.
See how the light shines round about his brow !
How mild and great he seems, with heavenly eyes !
Good fortune is it thus to meet the gods."

So,—thinking him divine,—Sujâta drew

Tremblingly nigh, and kissed the earth and said,
With sweet face bent, "Would that the Holy One
Inhabiting this grove, Giver of good,
Merciful unto me his handmaiden,
Vouchsafing now his presence, might accept

These our poor gifts of snowy curds, fresh made
With milk as white as new-carved ivory!"

Therewith into the golden bowl she poured
The curds and milk, and on the hands of Buddh
Dropped attar from a crystal flask—distilled
Out of the hearts of roses: and he ate,

Speaking no word, while the glad mother stood
In reverence apart. But of that meal
So wondrous was the virtue that our Lord
Felt strength and life return as though the nights
Of watching and the days of fast had passed
In dream, as though the spirit with the flesh
Shared that fine meat and plumed its wings anew,
Like some delighted bird at sudden streams
Weary with flight o'er endless wastes of sand,
Which laves the desert dust from neck and crest.
And more Sujâta worshipped, seeing our Lord
Grow fairer and his countenance more bright:
"Art thou indeed the God?" she lowly asked,
"And hath my gift found favour?"

But Buddh said,
"What is it thou dost bring me?"

"Holy One!"
Answered Sujâta, "from our droves I took
Milk of a hundred mothers, newly-calved,
And with that milk I fed fifty white cows,
And with their milk twenty-and-five, and then
With theirs twelve more, and yet again with theirs
The six noblest and best of all our herds.
That yield I boiled with sandal and fine spice
In silver lotas, adding rice, well grown

From chosen seed, set in new-broken ground,
So picked that every grain was like a pearl.
This did I of true heart, because I vowed
Under thy tree, if I should bear a boy
I would make offering for my joy, and now
I have my son, and all my life is bliss!"

Softly our Lord drew down the crimson fold,
And, laying on the little head those hands
Which help the worlds, he said, "Long be thy bliss!
And lightly fall on him the load of life!
For thou hast holpen me who am no God,
But one, thy Brother; heretofore a Prince
And now a wanderer, seeking night and day
These six hard years that light which somewhere shines
To lighten all men's darkness, if they knew!
And I shall find the light; yea, now it dawned
Glorious and helpful, when my weak flesh failed
Which this pure food, fair Sister, hath restored,
Drawn manifold through lives to quicken life
As life itself passes by many births
To happier heights and purging off of sins.
Yet dost thou truly find it sweet enough
Only to live? Can life and love suffice?"

Answered Sujâta, "Worshipful! my heart

Is little, and a little rain will fill
The lily's cup which hardly moists the field.
It is enough for me to feel life's sun
Shine in my Lord's grace and my baby's smile,
Making the loving summer of our home.
Pleasant my days pass filled with household cares
From sunrise when I wake to praise the gods,
And give forth grain, and trim the tulsi-plant,
And set my handmaids to their tasks, till noon,
When my Lord lays his head upon my lap
Lulled by soft songs and wavings of the fan;
And so to supper-time at quiet eve,
When by his side I stand and serve the cakes.
Then the stars light their silver lamps for sleep,
After the temple and the talk with friends.
How should I not be happy, blest so much,
And bearing him this boy whose tiny hand
Shall lead his soul to Swarga, if it need?
For holy books teach when a man shall plant—
Trees for the travellers' shade, and dig a well
For the folks' comfort, and beget a son,
It shall be good for such after their death;
And what the books say that I humbly take,
Being not wiser than those great of old
Who spake with gods, and knew the hymns and charms,

And all the ways of virtue and of peace.
Also I think that good must come of good
And ill of evil—surely—unto all—
In every place and time—seeing sweet fruit
Groweth from wholesome roots, and bitter things
From poison stocks; yea, seeing, too, how spite
Breeds hate, and kindness friends, and patience peace
Even while we live; and when 'tis willed we die
Shall there not be as good a 'Then' as 'Now'?
Haply much better! since one grain of rice
Shoots a green feather gemmed with fifty pearls,
And all the starry champak's white and gold
Lurks in those little, naked, grey spring-buds.
Ah, Sir! I know there might be woes to bear
Would lay fond Patience with her face in dust.
If this my babe pass first I think my heart
Would break—almost I hope my heart would break;
That I might clasp him dead and wait my Lord—
In whatsoever world holds faithful wives—
Duteous, attending till his hour should come.
But if Death called Senâni, I should mount
The pile and lay that dear head in my lap,
My daily way, rejoicing when the torch
Lit the quick flame and rolled the choking smoke.
For it is written if an Indian wife

Die so, her love shall give her husband's soul
For every hair upon her head a crore
Of years in Swarga. Therefore fear I not;
And therefore, Holy Sir! my life is glad,
Nowise forgetting yet those other lives
Painful and poor, wicked and miserable,
Whereon the gods grant pity! But for me,
What good I see humbly I seek to do,
And live obedient to the law, in trust
That what will come, and must come, shall come well."

Then spake our Lord, "Thou teachest them who teach,
Wiser than wisdom in thy simple lore.
Be thou content to know not, knowing thus
Thy way of right and duty: grow, thou flower!
With thy sweet kind in peaceful shade—the light
Of Truth's high noon is not for tender leaves
Which must spread broad in other suns, and lift
In later lives a crowned head to the sky.
Thou who hast worshipped me, I worship thee!
Excellent heart! learned unknowingly,
As the dove is which flieth home by love.
In thee is seen why there is hope for man
And where we hold the wheel of life at will.

Peace go with thee, and comfort all thy days!
As thou accomplishest, may I achieve!
He whom thou thoughtest God bids thee wish this."

"Mayest thou achieve!" she said, with earnest eyes
Bent on her babe; who reached its tender hands
To Buddh—knowing, belike, as children know,
More than we deem, and reverencing our Lord;
But he arose—made strong with that pure meat—
And bent his footsteps where a great Tree grew,
The Bôdhi-tree (thenceforward in all years
Never to fade, and ever to be kept
In homage of the world), beneath whose leaves
It was ordained the Truth should come to Buddh:
Which now the Master knew; wherefore he went
With measured pace, steadfast, majestical,
Unto the Tree of Wisdom. Oh, ye Worlds!
Rejoice! our Lord wended unto the Tree!

Whom—as he passed into its ample shade,
Cloistered with columned dropping stems, and roofed
With vaults of glistering green—the conscious earth
Worshipped with waving grass and sudden flush
Of flowers about his feet. The forest-boughs
Bent down to shade him; from the river sighed
Cool wafts of wind laden with lotus-scents

Breathed by the water-gods. Large wondering eyes
Of woodland creatures—panther, boar, and deer—
At peace that eve, gazed on his face benign
From cave and thicket. From its cold cleft wound
The mottled deadly snake, dancing its hood
In honour of our Lord; bright butterflies
Fluttered their vans, azure and green and gold,
To be his fan-bearers; the fierce kite dropped
Its prey and screamed; the striped palm-squirrel raced
From stem to stem to see; the weaver bird
Chirped from her swinging nest; the lizard ran;
The koïl sang her hymn; the doves flocked round;
Even the creeping things were 'ware and glad.
Voices of earth and air joined in one song,
Which unto ears that hear said, "Lord and Friend!
Lover and Saviour! Thou who hast subdued
Angers and prides, desires and fears and doubts,
Thou that for each and all hast given thyself,
Pass to the Tree! The sad world blesseth thee
Who art the Buddh that shall assuage her woes.
Pass, Hailed and Honoured! strive thy last for us,
King and high Conqueror! thine hour is come;
This is the Night the ages waited for!"
Then fell the night, even as our Master sate
Under that Tree. But he who is the Prince

Of Darkness, Mara—knowing this was Buddh
Who should deliver men, and now the hour
When he should find the Truth and save the worlds—
Gave unto all his evil powers command.
Wherefore there trooped from every deepest pit
The fiends who war with Wisdom and the Light,
Arati, Trishna, Raga, and their crew
Of passions, horrors, ignorances, lusts,
The brood of gloom and dread ; all hating Buddh,
Seeking to shake his mind ; nor knoweth one,
Not even the wisest, how those fiends of Hell
Battled that night to keep the Truth from Buddh :
Sometimes with terrors of the tempest, blasts
Of demon-armies clouding all the wind
With thunder, and with blinding lightning flung
In jagged javelins of purple wrath
From splitting skies ; sometimes with wiles and words
Fair-sounding, 'mid hushed leaves and softened airs
From shapes of witching beauty ; wanton songs,
Whispers of love ; sometimes with royal allures
Of proffered rule ; sometimes with mocking doubts,
Making truth vain. But whether these befell
Without and visible, or whether Buddh
Strove with fell spirits in his inmost heart,
Judge ye :—I write what ancient books have writ.

The ten chief Sins came—Mara's mighty ones,
Angels of evil—Attavâda first,
The Sin of Self, who in the Universe
As in a mirror sees her fond face shown,
And, crying "I," would have the world say "I,"
And all things perish so if she endure.
"If thou be'st Buddh," she said, "let others grope
Lightless; it is enough that Thou art Thou
Changelessly; rise and take the bliss of gods
Who change not, heed not, strive not." But Buddh spake,
"The right in thee is base, the wrong a curse;
Cheat such as love themselves." Then came wan Doubt,
He that denies—the mocking Sin—and this
Hissed in the Master's ear, "All things are shows,
And vain the knowledge of their vanity;
Thou dost but chase the shadow of thyself;
Rise and go hence, there is no better way
Than patient scorn, nor any help for man,
Nor any staying of his whirling wheel."
But quoth our Lord, "Thou hast no part with me,
False Visikitcha! subtlest of man's foes."
And third came she who gives dark creeds their power,
Sîlabbat-paramâsa, sorceress,

Draped fair in many lands as lowly Faith,
But ever juggling souls with rites and prayers;
The keeper of those keys which lock up Hells
And open Heavens. "Wilt thou dare," she said,
"Put by our sacred books, dethrone our gods,
Unpeople all the temples, shaking down
That law which feeds the priests and props the realms?"
But Buddha answered, "What thou bidd'st me keep
Is form which passes, but the free Truth stands;
Get thee unto thy darkness." Next there drew
Gallantly nigh a braver Tempter, he,
Kama, the King of passions, who hath sway
Over the gods themselves, Lord of all loves,
Ruler of Pleasure's realm. Laughing he came
Unto the tree, bearing his bow of gold
Wreathed with red blooms, and arrows of desire
Pointed with five-tongued delicate flame, which stings
The heart it smites sharper than poisoned barb:
And round him came into that lonely place
Bands of bright shapes with heavenly eyes and lips
Singing in lovely words the praise of Love
To music of invisible sweet chords,
So witching, that it seemed the night stood still
To hear them, and the listening stars and moon
Paused in their orbits while these hymned to Buddh

Of lost delights, and how a mortal man
Findeth nought dearer in the Three wide worlds
Than are the yielded loving fragrant breasts
Of Beauty and the rosy breast-blossoms,
Love's rubies; nay, and toucheth nought more high
Than is that dulcet harmony of form
Seen in the lines and charms of loveliness,
Unspeakable, yet speaking, soul to soul,
Owned by the bounding blood, worshipped by will
Which leaps to seize it, knowing this is best,
This the true heaven where mortals are like gods,
Makers and Masters, this the gift of gifts
Ever renewed and worth a thousand woes.
For who hath grieved when soft arms shut him safe,
And all life melted to a happy sigh,
And all the world was given in one warm kiss?
So sang they with soft float of beckoning hands,
Eyes lighted with love-flames, alluring smiles;
In wanton dance their supple sides and limbs
Revealing and concealing like burst buds
Which tell their colour, but hide yet their hearts.
Never so matchless grace delighted eye
As troop by troop these midnight-dancers swept
Nearer the Tree, each daintier than the last,
Murmuring "O great Siddârtha! I am thine,

Taste of my mouth and see if youth is sweet!"
Also, when nothing moved our Master's mind,
Lo! Kama waved his magic bow, and lo!
The band of dancers opened, and a shape,
Fairest and stateliest of the throng, came forth
Wearing the guise of sweet Yasôdhara.
Tender the passion of those dark eyes seemed
Brimming with tears; yearning those outspread arms
Opened towards him; musical that moan
Wherewith the beauteous shadow named his name,
Sighing, "My Prince! I die for lack of thee!
What heaven hast thou found like that we knew
By bright Rohini in the Pleasure-house,
Where all these weary years I weep for thee?
Return, Siddârtha! ah! return. But touch
My lips again, but let me to thy breast
Once, and these fruitless dreams will end! Oh, look!
Am I not she thou lovedst?" But Buddh said,
"For that sweet sake of her thou playest thus,
Fair and false Shadow! is thy playing vain;
I curse thee not who wear'st a form so dear,
Yet as thou art so are all earthly shows.
Melt to thy void again!" Thereat, a cry
Thrilled through the grove, and all that comely rout

Faded with flickering wafts of flame, and trail
Of vaporous robes.
Next, under darkening skies
And noise of rising storm, came fiercer Sins,
The rearmost of the Ten; Patigha—Hate—
With serpents coiled about her waist, which suck
Poisonous milk from both her hanging dugs,
And with her curses mix their angry hiss.
Little wrought she upon that Holy One
Who with his calm eyes dumbed her bitter lips
And made her black snakes writhe to hide their fangs.
Then followed Ruparaga—Lust of days—
That sensual Sin which out of greed for life
Forgets to live; and next him Lust of Fame,
Nobler Aruparaga, she whose spell
Beguiles the wise, mother of daring deeds,
Battles and toils. And haughty Mano came,
The Fiend of Pride; and smooth Self-Righteousness,
Uddhachcha; and—with many a hideous band
Of vile and formless things, which crept and flapped
Toad-like and bat-like—Ignorance, the Dam
Of Fear and Wrong, Avidya, hideous hag,
Whose footsteps left the midnight darker, while
The rooted mountains shook, the wild winds howled,
The broken clouds shed from their caverns streams

Of levin-lighted rain; stars shot from heaven,
The solid earth shuddered as if one laid
Flame to her gaping wounds; the torn black air
Was full of whistling wings, of screams and yells,
Of evil faces peering, of vast fronts
Terrible and majestic, Lords of Hell
Who from a thousand Limbos led their troops
To tempt the Master.

But Buddh heeded not,
Sitting serene, with perfect virtue walled
As is a stronghold by its gates and ramps;
Also the Sacred Tree—the Bôdhi-tree—
Amid that tumult stirred not, but each leaf
Glistened as still as when on moonlit eves
No zephyr spills the gathering gems of dew;
For all this clamour raged outside the shade
Spread by those cloistered stems:

In the third watch,
The earth being still, the hellish legions fled,
A soft air breathing from the sinking moon—
Our Lord attained *Sammâ-sambuddh;* he saw,
By light which shines beyond our mortal ken,
The line of all his lives in all the worlds;
Far back, and farther back, and farthest yet,
Five hundred lives and fifty. Even as one,

At rest upon a mountain-summit, marks
His path wind up by precipice and crag,
Past thick-set woods shrunk to a patch; through bogs
Glittering false-green; down hollows where he toiled
Breathless; on dizzy ridges where his feet
Had well nigh slipped; beyond the sunny lawns,
The cataract, and the cavern, and the pool,
Backward to those dim flats wherefrom he sprang
To reach the blue; thus Buddha did behold
Life's upward steps long-linked, from levels low
Where breath is base, to higher slopes and higher
Whereon the ten great Virtues wait to lead
The climber skyward. Also, Buddha saw
How new life reaps what the old life did sow;
How where its march breaks off its march begins;
Holding the gain and answering for the loss;
And how in each life good begets more good,
Evil fresh evil; Death but casting up
Debit or credit, whereupon th' account
In merits or demerits stamps itself
By sure arithmic—where no tittle drops—
Certain and just, on some new-springing life;
Wherein are packed and scored past thoughts and
deeds,
Strivings and triumphs, memories and marks

Of lives foregone :

And in the middle watch
Our Lord attained *Abhidjna*—insight vast
Ranging beyond this sphere to spheres unnamed,
System on system, countless worlds and suns
Moving in splendid measures, band by band
Linked in division, one, yet separate,
The silver islands of a sapphire sea
Shoreless, unfathomed, undiminished, stirred
With waves which roll in restless tides of change.
He saw those Lords of Light who hold their worlds
By bonds invisible, how they themselves
Circle obedient round mightier orbs
Which serve profounder splendours, star to star
Flashing the ceaseless radiance of life
From centres ever shifting unto cirques
Knowing no uttermost. These he beheld
With unsealed vision, and of all those worlds,
Cycle on epicycle, all their tale
Of Kalpas, Mahakalpas—terms of time
Which no man grasps, yea, though he knew to count
The drops in Gunga from her springs to the sea,
Measureless unto speech—whereby these wax
And wane ; whereby each of this heavenly host
Fulfils its shining life, and darkling dies.

Sakwal by Sakwal, depths and heights he passed
Transported through the blue infinitudes,
Marking—behind all modes, above all spheres,
Beyond the burning impulse of each orb—
That fixed decree at silent work which wills
Evolve the dark to light, the dead to life,
To fulness void, to form the yet unformed,
Good unto better, better unto best,
By wordless edict; having none to bid,
None to forbid; for this is past all gods,
Immutable, unspeakable, supreme;
A Power which builds, unbuilds, and builds again,
Ruling all things accordant to the rule
Of virtue, which is beauty, truth, and use:
So that all things do well which serve the Power,
And ill which hinder; nay, the worm does well
Obedient to its kind; the hawk does well
Which carries bleeding quarries to its young;
The dewdrop and the star shine sisterly
Globing together in the common work;
And man who lives to die, dies to live well
So if he guide his ways by blamelessness
And earnest will to hinder not but help
All things both great and small which suffer life.
These did our Lord see in the middle watch.

But, when the fourth watch came, the secret came
Of Sorrow, which with evil mars the law,
As damp and dross hold back the goldsmith's fire.
Then was the Dukha-Satya opened him
First of the "Noble Truths;" how Sorrow is
Shadow to life, moving where life doth move;
Not to be laid aside until one lays
Living aside, with all its changing states,
Birth, growth, decay, love, hatred, pleasure, pain,
Being and doing. How that none strips off
These sad delights and pleasant griefs who lacks
Knowledge to know them snares; but he who knows
Avidya—Delusion—sets those snares,
Loves life no longer, but ensues escape.
The eyes of such a one are wide, he sees
Delusion breeds Sankhâra, Tendency
Perverse; Tendency Energy—Vidnnân—
Whereby comes Namarûpa, local Form
And Name and Bodiment, bringing the man
With senses naked to the sensible,
A helpless mirror of all shows which pass
Across his heart; and so Vedanâ grows—
'Sense-life'—false in its gladness, fell in sadness,
But sad or glad, the Mother of Desire,
Trishna, that thirst which makes the living drink

Deeper and deeper of the false salt waves
Whereon they float, pleasures, ambitions, wealth.
Praise, fame, or domination, conquest, love;
Rich meats and robes, and fair abodes and pride
Of ancient lines, and lust of days, and strife
To live, and sins that flow from strife, some sweet,
Some bitter. Thus Life's thirst quenches itself
With draughts which double thirst, but who is wise
Tears from his soul this Trishna, feeds his sense
No longer on false shows, files his firm mind
To seek not, strive not, wrong not; bearing meek
All ills which flow from foregone wrongfulness,
And so constraining passions that they die
Famished; till all the sum of ended life—
The *Karma*—all that total of a soul
Which is the things it did, the thoughts it had,
The 'Self' it wove—with woof of viewless time,
Crossed on the warp invisible of acts—
The outcome of him on the Universe,
Grows pure and sinless; either never more
Needing to find a body and a place,
Or so informing what fresh frame it takes
In new existence that the new toils prove
Lighter and lighter not to be at all,
Thus "finishing the Path;" free from Earth's cheats;

Released from all the Skandhas of the flesh ;
Broken from ties—from Upâdânas—saved
From whirling on the Wheel ; aroused and sane
As is a man wakened from hateful dreams.
Until—greater than Kings, than Gods more glad !—
The aching craze to live ends, and life glides—
Lifeless—to nameless quiet, nameless joy,
Blessed NIRVANA—sinless, stirless rest—
That change which never changes !
Lo ! the Dawn
Sprang with Buddh's victory ! lo ! in the East
Flamed the first fires of beauteous day, poured forth
Through fleeting folds of Night's black drapery.
High in the widening blue the herald-star
Faded to paler silver as there shot
Brighter and brightest bars of rosy gleam
Across the grey. Far off the shadowy hills
Saw the great Sun, before the world was 'ware,
And donned their crowns of crimson ; flower by flower
Felt the warm breath of Morn and 'gan unfold
Their tender lids. Over the spangled grass
Swept the swift footsteps of the lovely Light,
Turning the tears of Night to joyous gems,
Decking the earth with radiance, 'broidering
The sinking storm-clouds with a golden fringe,

Gilding the feathers of the palms, which waved
Glad salutation ; darting beams of gold
Into the glades ; touching with magic wand
The stream to rippled ruby ; in the brake
Finding the mild eyes of the antelopes
And saying "It is day !" in nested sleep
Touching the small heads under many a wing
And whispering "Children, praise the light of day !"
Whereat there piped anthems of all the birds,
The Köil's fluted song, the Bulbul's hymn,
The "morning, morning" of the painted thrush,
The twitter of the sunbirds starting forth
To find the honey ere the bees be out,
The grey crow's caw, the parrot's scream, the strokes
Of the green hammersmith, the myna's chirp,
The never-finished love-talk of the doves :
Yea ! and so holy was the influence
Of that high Dawn which came with victory
That, far and near, in homes of men there spread
An unknown peace. The slayer hid his knife ;
The robber laid his plunder back ; the shroff
Counted full tale of coins ; all evil hearts
Grew gentle, kind hearts gentler, as the balm
Of that divinest Daybreak lightened Earth.
Kings at fierce war called truce ; the sick men leaped

Laughing from beds of pain; the dying smiled
As though they knew that happy Morn was sprung
From fountains farther than the utmost East;
And o'er the heart of sad Yasôdhara,
Sitting forlorn at Prince Siddârtha's bed,
Came sudden bliss, as if love should not fail
Nor such vast sorrow miss to end in joy.
So glad the World was—though it wist not why—
That over desolate wastes went swooning songs
Of mirth, the voice of bodiless Prets and Bhuts
Foreseeing Buddh; and Devas in the air
Cried "It is finished, finished!" and the priests
Stood with the wondering people in the streets
Watching those golden splendours flood the sky,
And saying "There hath happed some mighty thing."
Also in Ran and Jungle grew that day
Friendship amongst the creatures; spotted deer
Browsed fearless where the tigress fed her cubs,
And cheetahs lapped the pool beside the bucks;
Under the eagle's rock the brown hares scoured
While his fierce beak but preened an idle wing;
The snake sunned all his jewels in the beam
With deadly fangs in sheath; the shrike let pass
The nestling-finch; the emerald halcyons
Sate dreaming while the fishes played beneath,

Nor hawked the merops, though the butterflies—
Crimson and blue and amber—flitted thick
Around his perch; the Spirit of our Lord
Lay potent upon man and bird and beast,
Even while he mused under that Bôdhi-tree,
Glorified with the Conquest gained for all,
And lightened by a Light greater than Day's.

Then he arose—radiant, rejoicing, strong—
Beneath the Tree, and lifting high his voice
Spake this, in hearing of all Times and Worlds:—

Anékajátisangsârang
Sandháwissang anibhisang
Gahakárakangawesanto
Dukkhájátipunappunang.

Gahakárakadithósi;
Punagehang nakáhasi;
Sabhátephásukhábhaggá,
Gahakútangwisang khitang;
Wisangkháragatang chittang;
Janhánangkhayamajhagá.

MANY A HOUSE OF LIFE
HATH HELD ME—SEEKING EVER HIM WHO WROUGHT
THESE PRISONS OF THE SENSES, SORROW-FRAUGHT;
SORE WAS MY CEASELESS STRIFE!

BUT NOW,
THOU BUILDER OF THIS TABERNACLE—THOU!
I KNOW THEE! NEVER SHALT THOU BUILD AGAIN
THESE WALLS OF PAIN,
NOR RAISE THE ROOF-TREE OF DECEITS, NOR LAY
FRESH RAFTERS ON THE CLAY;
BROKEN THY HOUSE IS, AND THE RIDGE-POLE SPLIT!
DELUSION FASHIONED IT!
SAFE PASS I THENCE—DELIVERANCE TO OBTAIN.

BOOK THE SEVENTH.

Book the Seventh.

SORROWFUL dwelt the King Suddhôdana
All those long years among the Sâkya Lords
Lacking the speech and presence of his Son;
Sorrowful sate the sweet Yasôdhara
All those long years, knowing no joy of life,
Widowed of him her living Liege and Prince.
And ever, on the news of some recluse
Seen far away by pasturing camel-men
Or traders threading devious paths for gain,
Messengers from the King had gone and come,
Bringing account of many a holy sage
Lonely and lost to home; but nought of him
The crown of white Kapilavastu's line,
The glory of her monarch and his hope,

The heart's content of sweet Yasôdhara,
Far-wandered now, forgetful, changed, or dead.

But on a day in the Wasanta-time,
When silver sprays swing on the mango-trees
And all the earth is clad with garb of spring,
The Princess sate by that bright garden-stream
Whose gliding glass, bordered with lotus-cups,
Mirrored so often in the bliss gone by
Their clinging hands and meeting lips. Her lids
Were wan with tears, her tender cheeks had thinned;
Her lips' delicious curves were drawn with grief;
The lustrous glory of her hair was hid—
Close-bound as widows use; no ornament
She wore, nor any jewel clasped the cloth—
Coarse, and of mourning-white—crossed on her breast.
Slow moved and painfully those small fine feet
Which had the roe's gait and the rose-leaf's fall
In old years at the loving voice of him.
Her eyes, those lamps of love,—which were as if
Sunlight should shine from out the deepest dark,
Illumining Night's peace with Daytime's glow—
Unlighted now, and roving aimlessly,
Scarce marked the clustering signs of coming Spring,
So the silk lashes drooped over their orbs.

In one hand was a girdle thick with pearls,
Siddârtha's—treasured since that night he fled—
(Ah, bitter Night! mother of weeping days!
When was fond Love so pitiless to love,
Save that this scorned to limit love by life?)
The other led her little son, a boy
Divinely fair, the pledge Siddârtha left—
Named Rahula—now seven years old, who tripped
Gladsome beside his mother, light of heart
To see the spring-blooms burgeon o'er the world.

So, while they lingered by the lotus-pools,
And, lightly laughing, Rahula flung rice
To feed the blue and purple fish; and she
With sad eyes watched the swiftly-flying cranes,
Sighing, "Oh! creatures of the wandering wing,
If ye shall light where my dear Lord is hid,
Say that Yasôdhara lives nigh to death
For one word of his mouth, one touch of him!"—
Thus, as they played and sighed—mother and child—
Came some among the damsels of the Court
Saying, "Great Princess! there have entered in
At the south gate merchants of Hastinpûr,
Tripusha called and Bhalluk, men of worth,
Long travelled from the loud sea's edge, who bring

Marvellous lovely webs pictured with gold,
Waved blades of gilded steel, wrought bowls in brass,
Cut ivories, spice, simples, and unknown birds,
Treasures of far-off peoples; but they bring
That which doth beggar these, for He is seen!
Thy Lord,—our Lord,—the hope of all the land—
Siddârtha! they have seen him face to face,
Yea, and have worshipped him with knees and brows,
And offered offerings; for he is become
All which was shown, a Teacher of the wise,
World-honoured, holy, wonderful; a Buddh
Who doth deliver men and save all flesh
By sweetest speech and pity vast as Heaven:
And, lo! he journeyeth hither, these do say."

Then—while the glad blood bounded in her veins
As Gunga leaps when first the mountain snows
Melt at her springs—uprose Yasôdhara
And clapped her palms, and laughed, with brimming tears
Beading her lashes. "Oh! call quick," she cried,
"These merchants to my purdah, for mine ears
Thirst like parched throats to drink their blessed news.
Go bring them in,—but, if their tale be true,
Say I will fill their girdles with much gold,

With gems that Kings shall envy: come ye too,
My girls, for ye shall have guerdon of this
If there be gifts to speak ny grateful heart."

So went those merchants to the Pleasure-House,
Full softly pacing through its golden ways
With naked feet, amid the peering maids,
Much wondering at the glories of the Court.
Whom, when they came without the purdah's folds,
A voice, tender and eager, filled and charmed
With trembling music, saying, "Ye are come
From far, fair Sirs! and ye have seen my Lord—
Yea, worshipped—for he is become a Buddh,
World-honoured, holy, and delivers men,
And journeyeth hither. Speak! for, if this be,
Friends are ye of my House, welcome and dear."

Then answer made Tripusha, "We have seen
That sacred Master, Princess! we have bowed
Before his feet; for who was lost a Prince
Is found a greater than the King of kings.
Under the Bôdhi-tree by Phalgû's bank
That which shall save the world hath late been wrought
By him,—the Friend of all, the Prince of all—
Thine most, High Lady! from whose tears men win

The comfort of this Word the Master speaks.
Lo! he is well, as one beyond all ills,
Uplifted as a god from earthly woes,
Shining with risen Truth, golden and clear.
Moreover as he entereth town by town,
Preaching those noble ways which lead to peace,
The hearts of men follow his path as leaves
Troop to the wind or sheep draw after one
Who knows the pastures. We ourselves have heard,
By Gaya in the green Tchîrnika grove,
Those wondrous lips and done them reverence:
He cometh hither ere the first rains fall."

Thus spake he, and Yasôdhara, for joy,
Scarce mastered breath to answer, "Be it well
Now and at all times with ye, worthy friends!
Who bring good tidings; but of this great thing
Wist ye how it befell?"

Then Bhalluk told
Such as the people of the valleys knew
Of that dread night of conflict, when the air
Darkened with fiendish shadows, and the earth
Quaked, and the waters swelled with Mara's wrath.
Also how gloriously that morning broke
Radiant with rising hopes for man, and how

The Lord was found rejoicing 'neath his Tree.
But many days the burden of release—
To be escaped beyond all storms of doubt,
Safe on Truth's shore—lay, spake he, on that heart
A golden load; for how shall men—Buddh mused—
Who love their sins and cleave to cheats of sense,
And drink of error from a thousand springs,
Having no mind to see, nor strength to break
The fleshly snare which binds them—how should such
Receive the Twelve Nidânas and the Law
Redeeming all, yet strange to profit by,
As the caged bird oft shuns its opened door?
So had we missed the helpful victory
If, in this earth without a refuge, Buddh,
Winning the way, had deemed it all too hard
For mortal feet and passed, none following him.
Yet pondered the compassion of our Lord;
But in that hour there rang a voice as sharp
As cry of travail, so as if the earth
Moaned in birth-throe, "*Naśyami aham bhû*
Naśyati lóka!" SURELY I AM LOST,
I AND MY CREATURES: then a pause, and next
A pleading sigh borne on the western wind,
"*Śruyatâm dharma, Bhagwat!*" OH, SUPREME!
LET THY GREAT LAW BE UTTERED! Whereupon

The Master cast his vision forth on flesh,
Saw who should hear and who must wait to hear,
As the keen Sun gilding the lotus-lakes
Seeth which buds will open to his beams
And which are not yet risen from their roots;
Then spake, divinely smiling, "Yea! I preach!
Whoso will listen let him learn the Law."

Afterwards passed he, said they, by the hills
Unto Benares, where he taught the Five,
Showing how birth and death should be destroyed,
And how man hath no fate except past deeds,
No Hell but what he makes, no Heaven too high
For those to reach whose passions sleep subdued.
This was the fifteenth day of Vaishya
Mid-afternoon, and that night was full moon.

But, of the Rishis, first Kaundinya
Owned the Four Truths and entered on the Paths;
And after him Bhadraka, Asvajit,
Basava, Mahanâma; also there
Within the Deer-park, at the feet of Buddh,
Yasad the Prince with nobles fifty-four,
Hearing the blessed word our Master spake,
Worshipped and followed; for there sprang up peace

And knowledge of a new time come for men
In all who heard, as spring the flowers and grass
When water sparkles through a sandy plain.

These sixty—said they—did our Lord send forth,
Made perfect in restraint and passion-free,
To teach the Way; but the World-honoured turned
South from the Deer-park and Isipatan
To Yashti and King Bimbisâra's realm,
Where many days he taught; and after these
King Bimbisâra and his folk believed,
Learning the law of love and ordered life.
Also he gave the Master, of free gift,—
Pouring forth water on the hands of Buddh,—
The Bamboo-Garden, named Wéluvana,
Wherein are streams and caves and lovely glades;
And the King set a stone there, carved with this:—

Yé dharma hetuppabhawá
Yesan hétun Tathágató;
Aha yesan cha yo nirodhó
Ewan wadi Maha Śamano.

"What life's course and cause sustain
These Tathâgato made plain;

What delivers from life's woe
That our Lord hath made us know."

And, in that Garden—said they—there was held
A high Assembly, where the Teacher spake
Wisdom and power, winning all souls which heard;
So that nine hundred took the yellow robe—
Such as the Master wears,—and spread his Law;
And this the gâthâ was wherewith he closed:—

Sabba pápassa akaranan;
Kusalassa upasampadá:
Sa chitta pariyodapanan;
Etan Budhánusásanan.

"Evil swells the debts to pay,
Good delivers and acquits;
Shun evil, follow good; hold sway
Over thyself. This is the Way."

Whom, when they ended, speaking so of him,
With gifts, and thanks which made the jewels dull,
The Princess recompensed. "But by what road
Wendeth my Lord?" she asked: the merchants said,
"Yôjans threescore stretch from the city-walls

To Rajagriha, whence the easy path
Passeth by Sona hither, and the hills.
Our oxen, treading eight slow koss a day,
Came in one moon."

Then the King, hearing word,
Sent nobles of the Court—well-mounted lords—
Nine separate messengers, each embassy
Bidden to say, "The King Suddhôdana—
Nearer the pyre by seven long years of lack,
Wherethrough he hath not ceased to seek for thee—
Prays of his son to come unto his own,
The Throne and people of this longing Realm,
Lest he shall die and see thy face no more.'
Also nine horsemen sent Yasôdhara
Bidden to say, "The Princess of thy House—
Rahula's mother—craves to see thy face
As the night-blowing moon-flower's swelling heart
Pines for the moon, as pale asôka-buds
Wait for a woman's foot: if thou hast found
More than was lost, she prays her part in this,
Rahula's part, but most of all thyself."
So sped the Sâkya Lords, but it befell
That each one, with the message in his mouth,
Entered the Bamboo-Garden in that hour
When Buddha taught his Law; and—hearing—each

Forgot to speak, lost thought of King and quest,
Of the sad Princess even ; only gazed
Eye-rapt upon the Master ; only hung
Heart-caught upon the speech, compassionate,
Commanding, perfect, pure, enlightening all,
Poured from those sacred lips. Look ! like a bee
Winged for the hive, who sees the môgras spread

And scents their utter sweetness on the air,
If he be honey-filled, it matters not ;
If night be nigh, or rain, he will not heed ;
Needs must he light on those delicious blooms
And drain their nectar ; so these messengers
One with another, hearing Buddha's words,
Let go the purpose of their speed, and mixed,
Heedless of all, amid the Master's train.

Wherefore the King bade that Udayi go—
Chiefest in all the Court, and faithfullest,
Siddârtha's playmate in the happier days—
Who, as he drew anear the garden, plucked
Blown tufts of tree-wool from the grove and sealed
The entrance of his hearing; thus he came
Safe through the lofty peril of the place,
And told the message of the King, and hers.

Then meekly bowed his head and spake our Lord
Before the people, "Surely I shall go!
It is my duty as it was my will;
Let no man miss to render reverence
To those who lend him life, whereby come means
To live and die no more, but safe attain
Blissful Nirvâna, if ye keep the Law,
Purging past wrongs and adding nought thereto,
Complete in love and lovely charities.
Let the King know and let the Princess hear
I take the way forewith." This told, the folk
Of white Kapilavastu and its fields
Made ready for the entrance of their Prince.
At the south gate a bright pavilion rose
With flower-wreathed pillars, and the walls of silk
Wrought on their red and green with woven gold.

Also the roads were laid with scented boughs
Of neem and mango, and full mussuks shed
Sandal and jasmine on the dust; and flags
Fluttered; and on the day when he should come
It was ordained how many elephants—
With silver howdahs and their tusks gold-tipped—
Should wait beyond the ford, and where the drums
Should boom "Siddârtha cometh!" where the lords
Should light and worship, and the dancing girls
Where they should strew their flowers, with dance
 and song,
So that the steed he rode might tramp knee-deep
In rose and balsam, and the ways be fair;
While the town rang with music and high joy.
This was ordained, and all men's ears were pricked
Dawn after dawn to catch the first drum's beat
Announcing, "Now he cometh!"
 But it fell—
Eager to be before—Yasôdhara
Rode in her litter to the city-walls
Where soared the bright pavilion. All around
A beauteous garden smiled—Nigrôdha named—
Shaded with bel-trees and the green-plumed dates,
New-trimmed and gay with winding walks and banks
Of fruits and flowers; for the southern road

Skirted its lawns, on this hand leaf and bloom,
On that the suburb-huts where base-borns dwelt
Outside the gates, a patient folk and poor,
Whose touch for Kshatriya and priest of Brahm
Were sore defilement. Yet those, too, were quick
With expectation, rising ere the dawn
To peer along the road, to climb the trees
At far-off trumpet of some elephant,
Or stir of temple-drum ; and when none came,
Busied with lowly chares to please the Prince ;
Sweeping their door-stones, setting forth their flags,
Stringing the fluted fig-leaves into chains,
New furbishing the Lingam, decking new
Yesterday's faded arch of boughs, but aye
Questioning wayfarers if any noise
Be on the road of great Siddârtha. These
The Princess marked with lovely languid eyes,
Watching, as they, the southward plain, and bent
Like them to listen if the passers gave
News of the path. So fell it she beheld
One slow approaching with his head close shorn,
A yellow cloth over his shoulder cast,
Girt as the hermits are, and in his hand
An earthen bowl, shaped melonwise, the which
Meekly at each hut-door he held a space,

Taking the granted dole with gentle thanks
And all as gently passing where none gave.
Two followed him wearing the yellow robe,
But he who bore the bowl so lordly seemed,
So reverend, and with such a passage moved,
With so commanding presence filled the air,
With such sweet eyes of holiness smote all,
That, as they reached him alms the givers gazed
Awestruck upon his face, and some bent down
In worship, and some ran to fetch fresh gifts
Grieved to be poor; till slowly, group by group,
Children and men and women drew behind
Into his steps, whispering with covered lips,
"Who is he? who? when looked a Rishi thus?"
But as he came with quiet footfall on
Nigh the pavilion, lo! the silken door
Lifted, and, all unveiled, Yasôdhara
Stood in his path crying, "Siddârtha! Lord!"
With wide eyes streaming and with close-clasped hands,
Then sobbing fell upon his feet, and lay.

Afterwards, when this weeping lady passed
Into the Noble Paths, and one had prayed
Answer from Buddha wherefore—being vowed
Quit of all mortal passion and the touch,

Flower-soft and conquering, of a woman's hands—
He suffered such embrace, the Master said:
"The greater beareth with the lesser love
So it may raise it unto easier heights.
Take heed that no man, being 'scaped from bonds,
Vexeth bound souls with boasts of liberty.
Free are ye rather that your freedom spread
By patient winning and sweet wisdom's skill.
Three eras of long toil bring Bodhisáts—
Who will be guides and help this darkling world—
Unto deliverance, and the first is named
Of deep 'Resolve,' the second of 'Attempt,'
The third of 'Nomination.' Lo! I lived
In era of Resolve, desiring good,
Searching for wisdom, but mine eyes were sealed.
Count the grey seeds on yonder castor-clump,
So many rains it is since I was Ram,
A merchant of the coast which looketh south
To Lanka and the hiding-place of pearls.
Also in that far time Yasôdhara
Dwelt with me in our village by the sea,
Tender as now, and Lukshmi was her name.
And I remember how I journeyed thence
Seeking our gain, for poor the household was
And lowly. Not the less with wistful tears

She prayed me that I should not part, nor tempt
Perils by land and water. 'How could love
Leave what it loved?' she wailed; yet, venturing, I
Passed to the Straits, and after storm and toil
And deadly strife with creatures of the deep,
And woes beneath the midnight and the noon,
Searching the wave I won therefrom a pearl
Moonlike and glorious, such as Kings might buy
Emptying their treasury. Then came I glad
Unto mine hills, but over all that land
Famine spread sore; ill was I stead to live
In journey home, and hardly reached my door—
Aching for food—with that white wealth of the sea
Tied in my girdle. Yet no food was there;
And on the threshold she for whom I toiled—
More than myself—lay with her speechless lips
Nigh unto death for one small gift of grain.
Then cried I, 'If there be who hath of grain,
Here is a kingdom's ransom for one life;
Give Lukshmi bread and take my moonlight pearl.'
Whereat one brought the last of all his hoard,
Millet—three seers—and clutched the beauteous thing.
But Lukshmi lived, and sighed with gathered life,
'Lo! thou didst love indeed!' I spent my pearl
Well in that life to comfort heart and mind

Else quite uncomforted ; but these pure pearls,
My last great gain, won from a deeper wave—
The Twelve Nidânas and the Law of Good--
Cannot be spent, nor dimmed, and most fulfil
Their perfect beauty being freeliest given.
For like as is to Meru yonder hill
Heaped by the little ants, and like as dew
Dropped in the footmark of a bounding roe
Unto the shoreless seas, so was that gift
Unto my present giving ; and so love—
Vaster in being free from toils of sense—
Was wisest stooping to the weaker heart ;
And so the feet of sweet Yasôdhara
Passed into peace and bliss, being softly led.'

But when the King heard how Siddârtha came
Shorn, with the mendicant's sad-coloured cloth,
And stretching out a bowl to gather orts
From base-borns' leavings, wrathful sorrow drave
Love from his heart. Thrice on the ground he spat,
Plucked at his silvered beard, and strode straight forth
Lackeyed by trembling lords. Frowning he clomb
Upon his war-horse, drove the spurs, and dashed,
Angered, through wondering streets and lanes of folk
Scarce finding breath to say, "The King! bow down!"

Ere the loud cavalcade had clattered by:
Which—at the turning by the Temple-wall,
Where the south gate was seen—encountered full
A mighty crowd; to every edge of it
Poured fast more people, till the roads were lost,
Blotted by that huge company which thronged
And grew, close following him whose look serene
Met the old King's. Nor lived the father's wrath
Longer than while the gentle eyes of Buddh
Lingered in worship on his troubled brows,
Then downcast sank, with his true knee, to earth
In proud humility. So dear it seemed
To see the Prince, to know him whole, to mark
That glory greater than of earthly state
Crowning his head, that majesty which brought
All men, so awed and silent, in his steps.
Nathless, the King broke forth, "Ends it in this
That great Siddârtha steals into his realm,
Wrapt in a clout, shorn, sandalled, craving food
Of low-borns, he whose life was as a God's?
My son! heir of this spacious power, and heir
Of Kings who did but clap their palms to have
What earth could give or eager service bring?
Thou should'st have come apparelled in thy rank,
With shining spears, and tramp of horse and foot.

Lo! all my soldiers camped upon the road,
And all my city waited at the gates;
Where hast thou sojourned through these evil years
Whilst thy crowned father mourned? and she, too, there
Lived as the widows use, foregoing joys;
Never once hearing sound of song or string,
Nor wearing once the festal robe, till now
When in her cloth of gold she welcomes home
A beggar-spouse in yellow remnants clad.
Son! why is this?"
"My Father!" came reply,
"It is the custom of my race."
"Thy race,"
Answered the King, "counteth a hundred thrones
From Maha Sammât, but no deed like this."

"Not of a mortal line," the Master said,
"I spake, but of descent invisible,
The Buddhas who have been and who shall be
Of these am I, and what they did I do,
And this, which now befalls, so fell before,
That at his gate a King in warrior-mail
Should meet his son, a Prince in hermit-weeds;
And that, by love and self-control, being more
Than mightiest Kings in all their puissance,

The appointed helper of the Worlds should bow—
As now do I—and with all lowly love
Proffer, where it is owed for tender debts,
The first-fruits of the treasure he hath brought;

Which now I proffer."

Then the King amazed
Inquired "What treasure?" and the Teacher took
Meekly the royal palm, and while they paced

Through worshipping streets—the Princess and the King
On either side—he told the things which make
For peace and pureness, those Four noble Truths
Which hold all wisdom as shores shut the seas,
Those eight right Rules whereby who will may walk—
Monarch or slave—upon the perfect Path
That hath its Stages Four and Precepts Eight,
Whereby whoso will live—mighty or mean,
Wise or unlearned, man, woman, young or old—
Shall, soon or late, break from the wheels of life,
Attaining blest Nirvâna. So they came
Into the Palace-porch, Suddhôdana
With brows unknit drinking the mighty words,
And in his own hand carrying Buddha's bowl,
Whilst a new light brightened the lovely eyes
Of sweet Yasôdhara and sunned her tears;
And that night entered they the Way of Peace.

Through worshipping streets—the Princess and the
King.

Ch[illegible]-founded teachings which undo
The pains and sorrows, those Four noble Truths
Whence born all wisdom—as Shares(?) the seat,
Thus: the Eight Rules whereby who will may walk—
Monarch or slave—upon the perfect Path
That hath its Stages Four and Precepts Eight,
Whereby whoso will live—mighty or mean,
Wise or unlearned, [illegible] young or old—
Shall, soon or [illegible] wheels of life,
Attaining bles[illegible]

Into the Pat[illegible]
With these comfort[illegible] mighty words,
And in his own [illegible] Buddha's Bowl,
Which ... newly [illegible] the lovely eyes
Of sweet Yasōdhara and stayed her tears;
And that night entered they the Way of Peace.

BOOK THE EIGHTH.

Book the Eighth.

A BROAD mead spreads by swift
Kohâna's bank
At Nagara; five days shall
bring a man
In ox-wain thither from Ben-
ares' shrines
Eastward and northward jour-
neying. The horns
Of white Himâla look upon the place,
Which all the year is glad with blooms, and girt
By groves made green from that bright streamlet's
wave.
Soft are its slopes and cool its fragrant shades,
And holy all the spirit of the spot
Unto this time: the breath of eve comes hushed
Over the tangled thickets, and high heaps
Of carved red stones cloven by root and stem

Of creeping fig, and clad with waving veil
Of leaf and grass. The still snake glistens forth
From crumbled work of lac and cedar-beams
To coil his folds there on deep-graven slabs;
The lizard dwells and darts o'er painted floors
Where Kings have paced; the grey fox litters safe
Under the broken thrones; only the peaks,
And stream, and sloping lawns, and gentle airs
Abide unchanged. All else, like all fair shows
Of life, are fled—for this is where it stood,
The city of Suddhôdana, the hill
Whereon, upon an eve of gold and blue,
At sinking sun Lord Buddha set himself
To teach the Law in hearing of his own.

Lo! ye shall read it in the Sacred Books
How, being met in that glad pleasaunce-place—
A garden in old days with hanging walks,
Fountains, and tanks, and rose-banked terraces
Girdled by gay pavilions and the sweep
Of stately palace-fronts—the Master sate
Eminent, worshipped, all the earnest throng
Watching the opening of his lips to learn
That wisdom which hath made our Asia mild;
Whereto four thousand lakhs of living souls

Witness this day. Upon the King's right hand
He sate, and round were ranged the Sâkya Lords
Ananda, Devadatta—all the Court:

Behind stood Seriyut and Mugallan, chiefs
Of the calm brethren in the yellow garb,
A goodly company. Between his knees
Rahula smiled, with wondering childish eyes
Bent on the awful face, while at his feet

Sate sweet Yasôdhara, her heartaches gone,
Foreseeing that fair love which doth not feed
On fleeting sense, that life which knows no age,
That blessed last of deaths when Death is dead,
His victory and hers. Wherefore she laid
Her hand upon his hands, folding around
He silver shoulder-cloth his yellow robe,
Nearest in all the world to him whose words
The Three Worlds waited for. I cannot tell
A small part of the splendid lore which broke
From Buddha's lips: I am a late-come scribe
Who love the Master and his love of men,
And tell this legend, knowing he was wise,
But have not wit to speak beyond the books;
And time hath blurred their script and ancient sense,
Which once was new and mighty, moving all.
A little of that large discourse I know
Which Buddha spake on the soft Indian eve;
So, too, I know it writ that they who heard
Were more—lakhs more—crores more—than could be
seen,
For all the Devas and the Dead thronged there,
Till Heaven was emptied to the seventh zone
And uttermost dark Hells opened their bars;
Also the daylight lingered past its time

In rose-leaf radiance on the watching peaks,
So that it seemed Night listened in the glens
And Noon upon the mountains; yea! they write,
The Evening stood between them like some maid
Celestial, love-struck, rapt; the smooth-rolled clouds
Her braided hair; the studded stars the pearls
And diamonds of her coronal; the moon
Her forehead-jewel, and the deepening dark
Her woven garments. 'Twas her close-held breath
Which came in scented sighs across the lawns
While our Lord taught, and, while he taught, who
heard—
Though he were stranger in the land, or slave,
High caste or low, come of the Aryan blood,
Or Mlech or Jungle-dweller—seemed to hear
What tongue his fellows talked. Nay, outside those
Who crowded by the river, great and small,
The birds and beasts and creeping things—'tis writ—
Had sense of Buddha's vast embracing love
And took the promise of his piteous speech;
So that their lives—prisoned in shape of ape,
Tiger, or deer, shagged bear, jackal, or wolf,
Foul-feeding kite, pearled dove, or peacock gemmed,
Squat toad, or speckled serpent, lizard, bat;
Yea, or of fish fanning the river-waves—

Touched meekly at the skirts of brotherhood
With man who hath less innocence than these,
And in mute gladness knew their bondage broke
Whilst Buddha spake these things before the King :—

OM, AMITAYA ! measure not with words
  Th' Immeasurable ; nor sink the string of thought
Into the Fathomless. Who asks doth err,
  Who answers, errs. Say nought !

The Books teach Darkness was, at first of all,
  And Brahm, sole meditating in that Night :
Look not for Brahm and the Beginning there !
  Nor him, nor any light

Shall any gazer see with mortal eyes,
  Or any searcher know by mortal mind ;
Veil after veil will lift—but there must be
  Veil upon veil behind.

Stars sweep and question not. This is enough
  That life and death and joy and woe abide ;
And cause and sequence, and the course of time,
  And Being's ceaseless tide,

Which, ever changing, runs, linked like a river
  By ripples following ripples, fast or slow—
The same yet not the same—from far-off fountain
  To where its waters flow

Into the seas. These, steaming to the Sun,
  Give the lost wavelets back in cloudy fleece
To trickle down the hills, and glide again;
  Having no pause or peace.

This is enough to know, the phantasms are;
  The Heavens, Earths, Worlds, and changes changing them,
A mighty whirling wheel of strife and stress
  Which none can stay or stem.

Pray not! the Darkness will not brighten! Ask
  Nought from the Silence, for it cannot speak!
Vex not your mournful minds with pious pains!
  Ah! Brothers, Sisters! seek

Nought from the helpless gods by gift and hymn,
  Nor bribe with blood, nor feed with fruits and cakes;
Within yourselves deliverance must be sought;
  Each man his prison makes.

Each hath such lordship as the loftiest ones ;
  Nay, for with Powers above, around, below,
As with all flesh and whatsoever lives,
  Act maketh joy and woe.

What hath been bringeth what shall be, and is,
  Worse—better—last for first and first for last :
The Angels in the Heavens of Gladness reap
  Fruits of a holy past :

The devils in the underworlds wear out
  Deeds that were wicked in an age gone by :
Nothing endures : fair virtues waste with time,
  Foul sins grow purged thereby.

Who toiled a slave may come anew a Prince
  For gentle worthiness and merit won ;
Who ruled a King may wander earth in rags
  For things done and undone.

Higher than Indra's ye may lift your lot,
  And sink it lower than the worm or gnat ;
The end of many myriad lives is this,
  The end of myriads that.

Only, while turns this wheel invisible,
  No pause, no peace, no staying-place can be;
Who mounts may fall, who falls will mount; the spokes
  Go round unceasingly!

* * * *

If ye lay bound upon the wheel of change,
  And no way were of breaking from the chain,
The Heart of boundless Being is a curse,
  The Soul of Things fell Pain.

Ye are not bound! the Soul of Things is sweet,
  The Heart of Being is celestial rest;
Stronger than woe is will: that which was Good
  Doth pass to Better—Best.

I, Buddh, who wept with all my brothers' tears,
  Whose heart was broken by a whole world's woe,
Laugh and am glad, for there is Liberty!
  Ho! ye who suffer! know

Ye suffer from yourselves. None else compels,
  None other holds you that ye live and die,
And whirl upon the wheel, and hug and kiss
  Its spokes of agony,

Its tire of tears, its nave of nothingness.
  Behold, I show you Truth! Lower than hell,
Higher than heaven, outside the utmost stars,
  Farther than Brahm doth dwell,

Before beginning, and without an end,
  As space eternal and as surety sure,
Is fixed a Power divine which moves to good,
  Only its laws endure.

This is its touch upon the blossomed rose,
  The fashion of its hand shaped lotus-leaves;
In dark soil and the silence of the seeds
  The robe of Spring it weaves;

That is its painting on the glorious clouds,
  And these its emeralds on the peacock's train;
It hath its stations in the stars; its slaves
  In lightning, wind, and rain.

Out of the dark it wrought the heart of man,
  Out of dull shells the pheasant's pencilled neck;
Ever at toil, it brings to loveliness
  All ancient wrath and wreck.

The grey eggs in the golden sun-bird's nest
  Its treasures are, the bees' six-sided cell
Its honey-pot ; the ant wots of its ways,
  The white doves know them well.

It spreadeth forth for flight the eagle's wings
  What time she beareth home her prey ; it sends
The she-wolf to her cubs ; for unloved things
  It findeth food and friends.

It is not marred nor stayed in any use,
  All liketh it ; the sweet white milk it brings
To mothers' breasts ; it brings the white drops, too,
  Wherewith the young snake stings.

The ordered music of the marching orbs
  It makes in viewless canopy of sky ;
In deep abyss of earth it hides up gold,
  Sards, sapphires, lazuli.

Ever and ever fetching secrets forth,
  It sitteth in the green of forest-glades
Nursing strange seedlings at the cedār's root,
  Devising leaves, blooms, blades.

It slayeth and it saveth, nowise moved
  Except unto the working out of doom;
Its threads are Love and Life; and Death and Pain
  The shuttles of its loom.

It maketh and unmaketh, mending all;
  What it hath wrought is better than had been;
Slow grows the splendid pattern that it plans
  Its wistful hands between.

This is its work upon the things ye see:
  The unseen things are more; men's hearts and minds,
The thoughts of peoples and their ways and wills,
  Those, too, the great Law binds.

Unseen it helpeth ye with faithful hands,
  Unheard it speaketh stronger than the storm.
Pity and Love are man's because long stress
  Moulded blind mass to form.

It will not be contemned of any one;
  Who thwarts it loses, and who serves it gains;
The hidden good it pays with peace and bliss,
  The hidden ill with pains.

It seeth everywhere and marketh all:
  Do right—it recompenseth! do one wrong—
The equal retribution must be made,
  Though DHARMA tarry long.

It knows not wrath nor pardon; utter-true
  Its measures mete, its faultless balance weighs;
Times are as nought, to-morrow it will judge,
  Or after many days.

By this the slayer's knife did stab himself;
  The unjust judge hath lost his own defender;
The false tongue dooms its lie; the creeping thief
  And spoiler rob, to render.

Such is the Law which moves to righteousness,
  Which none at last can turn aside or stay;
The heart of it is Love, the end of it
  Is Peace and Consummation sweet. Obey!

*   *   *   *

The Books say well, my Brothers! each man's life
  The outcome of his former living is;
The bygone wrongs bring forth sorrows and woes,
  The bygone right breeds bliss.

That which ye sow ye reap. See yonder fields!
The sesamum was sesamum, the corn
Was corn. The Silence and the Darkness knew!
So is a man's fate born.

He cometh, reaper of the things he sowed,
Sesamum, corn, so much cast in past birth;
And so much weed and poison-stuff, which mar
Him and the aching earth.

If he shall labour rightly, rooting these,
And planting wholesome seedlings where they grew,
Fruitful and fair and clean the ground shall be,
And rich the harvest due.

If he who liveth, learning whence woe springs,
Endureth patiently, striving to pay
His utmost debt for ancient evils done
In Love and Truth alway;

If making none to lack, he throughly purge
The lie and lust of self forth from his blood;
Suffering all meekly, rendering for offence
Nothing but grace and good;

If he shall day by day dwell merciful,
  Holy and just and kind and true ; and rend
Desire from where it clings with bleeding roots,
  Till love of life have end :

He—dying—leaveth as the sum of him
  A life-count closed, whose ills are dead and quit,
Whose good is quick and mighty, far and near,
  So that fruits follow it.

No need hath such to live as ye name life ;
  That which began in him when he began
Is finished : he hath wrought the purpose through
  Of what did make him Man.

Never shall yearnings torture him, nor sins
  Stain him, nor ache of earthly joys and woes
Invade his safe eternal peace ; nor deaths
  And lives recur. He goes

Unto NIRVÂNA. He is one with Life,
  Yet lives not. He is blest, ceasing to be.
OM, MANI PADME, OM ! the Dewdrop slips
  Into the shining sea !

* * * *

This is the doctrine of the KARMA. Learn!
  Only when all the dross of sin is quit,
Only when life dies like a white flame spent
  Death dies along with it.

Say not "I am," "I was," or "I shall be,"
  Think not ye pass from house to house of flesh
Like travellers who remember and forget,
  Ill-lodged or well-lodged. Fresh

Issues upon the Universe that sum
  Which is the lattermost of lives. It makes
Its habitation as the worm spins silk
  And dwells therein. It takes

Function and substance as the snake's egg hatched
  Takes scale and fang; as feathered reed-seeds fly
O'er rock and loam and sand, until they find
  Their marsh and multiply.

Also it issues forth to help or hurt.
  When Death the bitter murderer doth smite,
Red roams the unpurged fragment of him, driven
  On winds of plague and blight.

But when the mild and just die, sweet airs breathe ;
  The world grows richer, as if desert-stream
Should sink away to sparkle up again
  Purer, with broader gleam ;

So merit won winneth the happier age
  Which by demerit halteth short of end ;
Yet must this Law of Love reign King of all
  Before the Kalpas end.

What lets ?—Brothers ! the Darkness lets ! which breeds
  Ignorance, mazed whereby ye take these shows
For true, and thirst to have, and, having, cling
  To lusts which work you woes.

Ye that will tread the Middle Road, whose course
  Bright Reason traces and soft Quiet smoothes ;
Ye who will take the high Nirvâna-way,
  List the Four Noble Truths.

The First Truth is of *Sorrow*. Be not mocked !
  Life which ye prize is long-drawn agony :
Only its pains abide ; its pleasures are
  As birds which light and fly.

Ache of the birth, ache of the helpless days,
  Ache of hot youth and ache of manhood's prime;
Ache of the chill grey years and choking death,
  These fill your piteous time.

Sweet is fond Love, but funeral-flames must kiss
  The breasts which pillow and the lips which cling;
Gallant is warlike Might, but vultures pick
  The joints of chief and King.

Beauteous is Earth, but all its forest-broods
  Plot mutual slaughter, hungering to live;
Of sapphire are the skies, but when men cry
  Famished, no drops they give.

Ask of the sick, the mourners, ask of him
  Who tottereth on his staff, lone and forlorn,
"Liketh thee life?"—these say the babe is wise
  That weepeth, being born.

The Second Truth is *Sorrow's Cause.* What grief
  Springs of itself and springs not of Desire?
Senses and things perceived mingle and light
  Passion's quick spark of fire:

So flameth Trishna, lust and thirst of things.
  Eager ye cleave to shadows, dote on dreams ;
A false Self in the midst ye plant, and make
  A world around which seems ;

Blind to the heights beyond, deaf to the sound
  Of sweet airs breathed from far past Indra's sky ;
Dumb to the summons of the true life kept
  For him who false puts by.

So grow the strifes and lusts which make earth's war,
  So grieve poor cheated hearts and flow salt tears ;
So wax the passions, envies, angers, hates ;
  So years chase blood-stained years

With wild red feet. So, where the grain should grow,
  Spreads the birân-weed with its evil root
And poisonous blossoms ; hardly good seeds find
  Soil where to fall and shoot ;

And, drugged with poisonous drink, the soul departs,
  And, fierce with thirst to drink, Karma returns ;
Sense-struck again the sodden Self begins,
  And new deceits it earns.

The Third is *Sorrow's Ceasing.* This is peace
  To conquer love of self and lust of life,
To tear deep-rooted passion from the breast,
  To still the inward strife;

For love to clasp Eternal Beauty close;
  For glory to be Lord of self; for pleasure
To live beyond the gods; for countless wealth
  To lay up lasting treasure

Of perfect service rendered, duties done
  In charity, soft speech, and stainless days:
These riches shall not fade away in life,
  Nor any death dispraise.

Then Sorrow ends, for Life and Death have ceased;
  How should lamps flicker when their oil is spent?
The old sad count is clear, the new is clean;
  Thus hath a man content.

* * * *

The Fourth Truth is *The Way.* It openeth wide,
  Plain for all feet to tread, easy and near,
The *Noble Eightfold Path;* it goeth straight
  To peace and refuge. Hear!

Manifold tracks lead to yon sister-peaks
  Around whose snows the gilded clouds are curled;
By steep or gentle slopes the climber comes
  Where breaks that other world.

Strong limbs may dare the rugged road which storms,
  Soaring and perilous, the mountain's breast;
The weak must wind from slower ledge to ledge,
  With many a place of rest.

So is the Eightfold Path which brings to peace;
  By lower or by upper heights it goes.
The firm soul hastes, the feeble tarries. All
  Will reach the sunlit snows.

The First good level is *Right Doctrine.* Walk
  In fear of Dharma, shunning all offence;
In heed of Karma, which doth make man's fate;
  In lordship over sense.

The Second is *Right Purpose.* Have good-will
  To all that lives, letting unkindness die
And greed and wrath; so that your lives be made
  Like soft airs passing by.

The Third is *Right Discourse.* Govern the lips
  As they were palace-doors, the King within;
Tranquil and fair and courteous be all words
  Which from that presence win.

The Fourth is *Right Behaviour.* Let each act
  Assoil a fault or help a merit grow:
Like threads of silver seen through crystal beads
  Let love through good deeds show.

Four higher roadways be. Only those feet
  May tread them which have done with earthly things,
Right Purity, *Right Thought*, *Right Loneliness*,
  Right Rapture. Spread no wings

For Sunward flight, thou soul with unplumed vans!
  Sweet is the lower air, and safe and known
The homely levels; only strong ones leave
  The nest each makes his own.

Dear is the love, I know, of Wife and Child;
  Pleasant the friends and pastimes of your years,
Fruitful of good Life's gentle charities;
  Firm-set, though false, its fears.

Live—ye who must—such lives as live on these ;
  Make golden stair-ways of your weakness ; rise
By daily sojourn with those phantasies
  To lovelier verities.

So shall ye pass to clearer heights and find
  Easier ascents and lighter loads of sins,
And larger will to burst the bonds of sense,
  Entering the Path. Who wins

To such commencement hath the *First Stage* touched,
  He knows the Noble Truths, the Eightfold Road :
By few or many steps such shall attain
  NIRVÂNA'S blest abode.

Who standeth at the *Second Stage*, made free
  From doubts, delusions, and the inward strife,
Lord of all lusts, quit of the priests and books,
  Shall live but one more life.

Yet onward lies the *Third Stage* : purged and pure
  Hath grown the stately spirit here, hath risen
To love all living things in perfect peace.
  His life at end, life's prison

Is broken. Nay, there are who surely pass
  Living and visible to utmost goal
By *Fourth Stage* of the Holy ones—the Buddhs—
  And they of stainless soul.

Lo! like fierce foes slain by some warrior,
  Ten sins along these Stages lie in dust,
The Love of Self, False Faith, and Doubt are three,
  Two more Hatred and Lust.

Who of these Five is conqueror hath trod
  Three stages out of Four: yet there abide
The Love of Life on earth, Desire for Heaven,
  Self-Praise, Error, and Pride.

As one who stands on yonder snowy horn
  Having nought o'er him but the boundless blue,
So, these sins being slain, the man is come
  NIRVÂNA's verge unto.

Him the Gods envy from their lower seats;
  Him the Three Worlds in ruin should not shake;
All life is lived for him, all deaths are dead;
  Karma will no more make

New houses. Seeking nothing, he gains all;
  Foregoing self, the Universe grows "I:"
If any teach NIRVANA is to cease,
  Say unto such they lie.

If any teach NIRVANA is to live,
  Say unto such they err; not knowing this,
Nor what light shines beyond their broken lamps,
  Nor lifeless, timeless, bliss.

Enter the path! There is no grief like Hate!
  No pains like passion, no deceit like sense!
Enter the path! far hath he gone whose foot
  Treads down one fond offence.

Enter the Path! There spring the healing streams
  Quenching all thirst! there bloom th' immortal flowers
Carpeting all the way with joy! there throng
  Swiftest and sweetest hours!

* * * *

More is the treasure of the Law than gems;
  Sweeter than comb its sweetness; its delights
Delightful past compare. Thereby to live
  Hear the *Five Rules* aright:—

Kill not—for Pity's sake—and lest ye slay
The meanest thing upon its upward way.

Give freely and receive, but take from none
By greed, or force, or fraud, what is his own.

Bear not false witness, slander not, nor lie;
Truth is the speech of inward purity.

Shun drugs and drinks which work the wit abuse;
Clear minds, clean bodies, need no Sôma juice.

Touch not thy neighbour's wife, neither commit
Sins of the flesh unlawful and unfit.

These words the Master spake of duties due
To father, mother, children, fellows, friends;
Teaching how such as may not swiftly break
The clinging chains of sense—whose feet are weak
To tread the higher road—should order so
This life of flesh that all their hither days
Pass blameless in discharge of charities
And first true footfalls in the Eightfold Path;

Living pure, reverent, patient, pitiful;
Loving all things which live even as themselves;
Because what falls for ill is fruit of ill
Wrought in the past, and what falls well of good;
And that by howsomuch the householder
Purgeth himself of self and helps the world,
By so much happier comes he to next stage,
In so much bettered being. This he spake;
As also long before, when our Lord walked
By Rajagriha in the bamboo-grove:
For on a dawn he walked there and beheld
The householder Singâla, newly bathed,
Bowing himself with bare head to the earth,
To Heaven, and all four quarters; while he threw
Rice, red and white, from both hands. "Wherefore thus
Bowest thou, Brother?" said the Lord; and he,
"It is the way, Great Sir! our fathers taught
At every dawn, before the toil begins,
To hold off evil from the sky above
And earth beneath, and all the winds which blow."
Then the World-honoured spake: "Scatter not rice,
But offer loving thoughts and acts to all:
To parents as the East, where rises light;
To teachers as the South, whence rich gifts come;

To wife and children as the West, where gleam
Colours of love and calm, and all days end;
To friends and kinsmen and all men as North;
To humblest living things beneath, to Saints
And Angels and the blessed Dead above:
So shall all evil be shut off, and so
The six main quarters will be safely kept."

But to his Own, Them of the yellow robe—
Those who, as wakened eagles, soar with scorn
From life's low vale, and wing towards the Sun—
To these he taught the Ten Observances
The *Dasa-Sîl*, and how a mendicant
Must know the *Three Doors* and the *Triple Thoughts;*
The *Sixfold States of mind;* the *Fivefold Powers;*
The *Eight High Gates of Purity;* the *Modes*
Of Understanding; Iddhi; Upekshâ;
The *Five Great Meditations*, which are food
Sweeter than Amrit for the holy soul;
The *Jhânas* and the *Three Chief Refuges.*
Also he taught his Own how they should dwell;
How live, free from the snares of love and wealth;
What eat and drink and carry—three plain cloths,—
Yellow, of stitched stuff, worn with shoulder bare—
A girdle, almsbowl, strainer. Thus he laid

The great foundations of our Sangha well,
That noble Order of the Yellow Robe
Which to this day standeth to help the World.

So all that night he spake, teaching the Law;
And on no eyes fell sleep—for they who heard
Rejoiced with tireless joy. Also the King,
When this was finished, rose upon his throne
And with bared feet bowed low before his Son
Kissing his hem; and said, "Take me, O Son!
Lowest and least of all thy Company."
And sweet Yasôdhara, all happy now,—
Cried "Give to Rahula—thou Blessed One!
The Treasure of the Kingdom of thy Word
For his inheritance." Thus passed these Three
Into the Path.

Here endeth what I write
Who love the Master for his love of us.
A little knowing, little have I told
Touching the Teacher and the Ways of Peace.
Forty-five rains thereafter showed he those
In many lands and many tongues, and gave
Our Asia Light, that still is beautiful,
Conquering the world with spirit of strong grace:
All which is written in the holy Books,
And where he passed, and what proud Emperors
Carved his sweet words upon the rocks and caves:
And how—in fulness of the times—it fell
The Buddha died, the great Tathâgato,
Even as a man 'mongst men, fulfilling all:
And how a thousand thousand lakhs since then
Have trod the Path which leads whither he went
Unto NIRVÂNA, where the Silence lives.

AH! BLESSED LORD! OH, HIGH DELIVERER!
FORGIVE THIS FEEBLE SCRIPT, WHICH DOTH THEE WRONG,
MEASURING WITH LITTLE WIT THY LOFTY LOVE.
AH! LOVER! BROTHER! GUIDE! LAMP OF THE LAW!
I TAKE MY REFUGE IN THY NAME AND THEE!
I TAKE MY REFUGE IN THY LAW OF GOOD!
I TAKE MY REFUGE IN THY ORDER! *OM!*
THE DEW IS ON THE LOTUS!—RISE, GREAT SUN!
AND LIFT MY LEAF AND MIX ME WITH THE WAVE
OM MANI PADME HUM, THE SUNRISE COMES!
THE DEWDROP SLIPS INTO THE SHINING SEA!

THE END

PRINTED BY BALLANTYNE, HANSON AND CO.
EDINBURGH AND LONDON.